T4-AJV-985

Bea Lewis is a nutrition and food writer for *Newsday*, a major New York newspaper, where her informative articles and delicious low-fat recipes have helped many thousands of readers enjoy a heart-healthy lifestyle. The author is married and the mother of three grown daughters. She is especially proud of her cholesterol level—a healthy 175!

Peter O. Kwiterovich, M.D., is director of the Lipid Research Clinic at Johns Hopkins School of Medicine, Baltimore, Maryland, and author of *Beyond Cholesterol: The Johns Hopkins Complete Guide for Avoiding Heart Disease*. He is also a member of the expert panel of the National Cholesterol Conference on Lowering Blood Cholesterol to Prevent Heart Disease which has recommended a prudent, low-cholesterol, low-saturated fat diet for all healthy American children over two years old.

Other Quick and Easy Cholesterol Handbooks
from Avon Books

THE QUICK AND EASY CHOLESTEROL & CALORIE COUNTER
QUICK AND EASY RECIPES TO LOWER YOUR CHOLESTEROL

QUICK AND EASY LOW-FAT, LOW-CHOLESTEROL RECIPES KIDS WILL LOVE

BEA LEWIS

Foreword by Peter O. Kwiterovich, M.D.

A LYNN SONBERG BOOK

AVON BOOKS ◆ NEW YORK

To my children, the present;
to my grandchildren, the future

AVON BOOKS
A division of
The Hearst Corporation
105 Madison Avenue
New York, New York 10016

Contents

Foreword

If you are one of the millions of parents who are wondering what they should be feeding their children, this book is for you. Bea Lewis provides some of the most creative recipes for youngsters that I have seen. Not only are they delicious and appealing, but they are low in saturated fat and cholesterol and packed full of important nutrients such as proteins, minerals, vitamins, and fiber.

I believe you will find Bea Lewis's breakfast suggestions a welcome change from the usual humdrum selections that parents rely on. The easy-to-prepare recipes will provide children with delicious and nutritious meals to start their day.

Many times school lunches are too high in fat and cholesterol. Have you wondered how you can get around this problem? This book is extremely helpful for those of you who wish to pack your children a healthier lunch.

Too often I find as a pediatrician that parents who try to modify their child's diet in terms of its total-fat, saturated-fat, and cholesterol content eliminate snacks. This is not a good idea because up to 20 percent of a child's calories comes from snacks. Calories are important for a child to grow normally. Bea Lewis provides an incredible array of creative, helpful snacks. These are supplemented by an equally appealing series of recipes and suggestions for birthday parties and holidays.

Finally, there are a number of appealing and quick suggestions for dinner. Bea Lewis puts them together with flair, and her general suggestions about "bringing the family back to the dinner table" reflect her love and devotion as a mother.

As if all this were not enough, everything in the book is

presented in an upbeat, clear, and enjoyable style that reflects the author's experience as a reporter for *Newsday*.

Clearly, this book will help you in day-to-day living to provide your children with the foods they need for heart-healthy living. The time has come to change the diet of American children to a more prudent, low-fat cuisine.

Recommendations from the National Cholesterol Conference on Lowering Blood Cholesterol to Prevent Heart Disease, from the recent Population Panel of the National Cholesterol Education Campaign, and from the American Heart Association have all included a prudent, low-cholesterol, low-saturated-fat diet for all healthy American children above the age of two years. If your child has a cholesterol problem these recipes are also appropriate on a low-saturated-fat, low-cholesterol diet. This book is not meant to provide an in-depth explanation of cholesterol and nutrition. Such information is available elsewhere in books such as *Beyond Cholesterol*.

I know you will find *Quick and Easy Low-Fat Low-Cholesterol Recipes Kids Will Love* enjoyable and tremendously useful. Your children will love you for it.

Peter O. Kwiterovich, M.D.
Director, Lipid Research Clinic
Johns Hopkins School of Medicine
Baltimore, Maryland

WHY ALL THE FUSS ABOUT CHOLESTEROL?

By now, most of us know that high levels of blood cholesterol increase our chance of developing heart disease, America's number one killer. We also know that high-cholesterol levels are a result of eating the foods we love—burgers, fries, pepperoni pizza, and lots of creamy pies—foods rich in fat and cholesterol that clog our arteries and lead to heart attack and stroke.

While health-conscious grown-ups nationwide are struggling to change their eating habits, researchers are turning to the diets of our young, hoping thereby to ward off health problems by encouraging a heart-smart diet during the childhood years when lasting eating habits are formed.

Today a startling number of youngsters are at risk. High cholesterol from a fatty diet is a problem that a child won't outgrow unless something is done about it, and one that tends to escalate with time. The following statistics, based on findings of pediatric scientists, are truly disturbing.

- one out of four children between the ages of two and eighteen has a higher than desirable cholesterol levels

- about one in twenty American youngsters has an exceedingly high cholesterol level—greater than 200 mg/dl

- children as young as two years can begin to develop a high cholesterol level

Whether your youngster already has high cholesterol, or whether you want to prevent the problem in the first place,

1

learning to eat the heart-smart way is important for all children over the age of two years. Before the age of two, children need more fat for proper growth and development. While a few experts think a heart-smart diet isn't necessary until the age of four or five, all experts agree that the diet for good health is one that emphasizes foods rich in complex carbohydrates, like whole grain cereals, fruits, vegetables, beans, potatoes, pasta, and breads in addition to lean meats and low-fat dairy products.

If we as a nation put our children on heart-healthy diets, and if the children follow this diet throughout life, it is estimated that the cholesterol level of the average American adult (which is now around 210 mg/dl) could drop by 10 percent or more to the recommended level for adults of 200 mg/dl—or less. And for every 10 percent drop in cholesterol, the risk of heart attack drops 20 percent.

It is in our early years that we form lasting eating habits. Our youngsters can learn to enjoy, say, a bowl of vegetable soup and whole grain bread instead of a hot dog for lunch, or a cup of low-fat yogurt and some fruit as an after-school snack rather than nachos or fries. If your child learns good eating habits at an early age, chances are that he or she will continue to choose healthy foods as a grown-up.

It is up to us parents to provide healthy foods for our children and to encourage a heart-smart eating style. Not an easy task. Still, it can be done, and this book will show you how. In the pages that follow, you'll find easy-to-follow advice on healthy eating, including daily meal plans and tips on how to remove excess fat from your child's diet. We'll help you stock the larder and learn to read food labels, and we'll teach you how to make quick meals, snacks, and desserts chock-full of good nutrition. Whether you're preparing everyday meals for your kids or cooking for special occasions like birthdays and holidays, we'll show you simple tricks that will turn fatty fare into healthful foods kids will love.

You might be surprised to learn that just a few easy changes—for example, switching from whole milk to milk containing 1 percent fat, eating more skinless poultry and

fish, and snacking on low-fat yogurt instead of ice cream—
can cut your child's daily fat intake by 30 percent! You can
still make his or her favorite cake or cookies, but we'll show
you low-fat, low-cholesterol versions.* This book contains
heart-healthy delicious dishes with kid appeal. We've included all the basics—breakfast ideas, brown bag lunches,
healthful soups, and main dishes—plus we've also empha-
sized snack foods like healthy desserts and cookies, because
we know how kids really eat. It makes a world of difference,
nutritionally speaking, if your kid replaces potato chips with
low-fat munchies like our Fruity Popcorn on page 98.

I know from experience that kids will eat heart-healthy
foods if you know how to prepare and present them. As the
nutrition writer for *Newsday,* a major New York newspaper,
I have written about healthful eating for years, gathering
tips and suggestions from the experts. And I have learned
to apply healthful principles in my daily home life. As the
mother of three daughters, I have come to learn what foods
are popular—and unpopular!—with kids. I have even
brought down my own children's cholesterol levels, using
changes in diet alone. My daughter Laurie's serum cholesterol went from an exceedingly high level of more than 200
mg/dl at age ten to well below 160.

I can't wait to get you started on a heart-healthy diet. But
don't rush out to make the changes overnight. Quick changes
may backfire. It happened to me. I remember coming home
one night and, in my desire to be a good mother, I threw
boxfuls of high-fat cookies that had been popular afternoon
snacks for years into the garbage. Worse, I did so with little
explanation and no delicious substitutes. Not surprisingly,
my children solved the problem by having their cookies at
their friends' houses instead—not much of an improvement!

Most experts advise parents to make changes gradually.
Above all, don't become obsessed. A cheeseburger is not
life threatening in the short run, though a steady diet of
them may affect your child's heart and arteries over the

*If your child has an elevated cholesterol of 200 mg/dl or higher his
diet should be planned by a registered dietitian, one recommended by your
child's physician.

years. Instead of switching from whole milk to skim or low-fat milk overnight, mix whole and low-fat milk until your child makes a comfortable adjustment. Or start with low-fat chocolate milk! Aim for progress, not perfection, and you'll be rewarded with a gradual acceptance of healthier eating styles by the entire family.

WHAT YOU NEED TO KNOW ABOUT CHOLESTEROL TESTING

Cholesterol screening for adults has been recommended for years, but today people are actually paying attention to the test results. Now adult Americans everywhere, urged by a major public health campaign to "know the score," have taken the trouble to get tested and learn their cholesterol count, which experts generally agree is a major risk factor in the development of heart disease. (Heredity, cigarette smoking, high blood pressure, and diabetes also can increase the risks.)

The attention of the medical community has now turned to our children. Currently the American Heart Association recommends cholesterol screening for children over the age of two years whose parents or grandparents had or have high cholesterol levels; early signs of cardiovascular disease; or a history of sudden heart attack, stroke, or other signs of heart disease. More and more pediatricians are recommending cholesterol screening for all children over the age of two, feeling it is the prudent course.

How can you find out if your pediatrician will check your child's cholesterol level? Just ask. In many offices a simple finger-prick test can be done, although some doctors may want to analyze a blood sample, which is considered a more reliable means of testing. Most doctors agree that more than one test should be taken before major dietary restrictions are recommended. However, a heart-healthy diet is appropriate for *everyone*.

What should your child's cholesterol level be? Here are the guidelines:

	TOTAL CHOLESTEROL	LDL* CHOLESTEROL
Desirable:	less than 170 mg/dl	less than 110 mg/dl
Borderline:	175 to 199 mg/dl	110 to 130 mg/dl
High:	200 mg/dl or higher	130 mg/dl or higher

In the next section we'll explain how the right diet can help keep your child's cholesterol level low and decrease his or her risk of developing high cholesterol as an adult.

HEART-SMART GUIDELINES FOR YOUR CHILD

1. *Keep it lean.* Reduce the total fat in your child's diet to 30 percent of his or her daily calories, with no more than 10 percent coming from saturated fat. Right now, most of us eat a diet in which 35 to 40 percent of the calories come from fat, with about 15 to 20 percent from saturated fat. Reduce your child's cholesterol consumption to 300 milligrams a day or less, or 100 milligrams for every 1000 calories consumed. Right now many children eat about 400 milligrams a day. If all this sounds a little technical, take heart—we'll show you what to do to get on the right track.

2. *Take five for better health.* Eat more fruits and vegetables, at least five servings a day.

3. *Take two for strong bones.* Drink at least two or three cups of low-fat milk or the equivalent of low-fat dairy-rich foods—low-fat yogurt, low-fat or skim milk cheeses, nonfat dry milk, part-skim milk ricotta cheese, etc.

4. *Keep tabs on protein.* Limit your child's intake to 5 to 7 ounces a day of lean meats, skinless poultry, fish, or meat alternatives. A 3-ounce serving is about the size of a deck of cards.

5. *Stay on the slim side.* Help your youngsters maintain a healthy weight for their height by eating a balanced diet

---

*There are two types of cholesterol: high-density lipoproteins (HDL)— "good" cholesterol—and low-density lipoproteins (LDL)—"bad" cholesterol. High levels of low-density lipoproteins are undesirable because they deposit excess cholesterol on artery walls. On the other hand, high-density lipoproteins help carry cholesterol back to the liver for disposal.

and getting lots of exercise. For some of the eleven million overweight youngsters—one in five—excercise alone may help reduce overweight and cholesterol levels.

6. *Go with the grain.* Introduce children to foods rich in complex carbohydrates. Serve more potatoes, whole grain breads and cereals, and try out whole grains such as kasha, barley, bulgur wheat, and brown rice.

7. *Reach for fiber.* Try out some recipes using foods rich in soluble fiber, the type of fiber that researchers say may help lower cholesterol levels. Encourage oat bran in muffins, rice bran in cookies. Add beans to salad, soup, and tacos. Try some prunes; encourage apples, oranges, and carrots.

8. *Go easy with the salt shaker.* Taste before you shake; go easy with processed and packaged foods that are high in sodium.

HOW TO EAT THE HEART-SMART WAY

The following chart provides more detailed help on how to translate the heart-smart guidelines on pages 5–6 into every day food choices. It is geared to the needs of an average eight to ten year old.

Food Group	Acceptable	Avoid or Use Sparingly
meat, poultry, fish, beans, nuts, eggs Servings: 5 to 6 ounces a day	chicken, turkey, veal (except the breast), fish, shellfish* (clams, crab, oysters, scallops), lean meats, egg whites, specially processed low-fat luncheon meats	duck, goose, heavily marbled meats, luncheon meats, bacon, sausage, ham, frank-furters, organ meats egg yolks (limit to four times per week —includes yolks used in cooking)

*Shrimp and lobster are moderately high in cholesterol, although low in fat.

Food Group	Acceptable	Avoid or Use Sparingly
meat, poultry, fish, beans, nuts, eggs *(cont.)*	dry beans and peas such as: kidney beans, lima beans, vegetarian-style baked beans, pinto beans, lentils, chick peas, split peas, navy beans soybean curd (tofu), natural peanut butter, cholesterol-free egg substitutes	
vegetables (canned, fresh or frozen) servings: 4 or more a day	all varieties	avoid fried or served in cream, butter, or cheese sauces
fruits (canned, fresh and frozen) servings: 4 or more		
breads and cereals servings: 5 or more a day	bread made with a minimum of saturated fat, such as: whole wheat, enriched white, French, Italian, oatmeal, rye, pumpernickel, English muffins, pita pasta, cereal, rice, melba toast, rice cakes, matzos, pretzels,	pastries, butter rolls, commercial biscuits, muffins, donuts, cakes, egg breads, cheese breads, commercial mixes containing dried eggs and whole milk. Many of these products are made with saturated fat (lard, butter, suet, palm oil, palm kernel,

Food Group	Acceptable	Avoid or Use Sparingly
breads and cereals *(cont.)*	air-popped popcorn, water bagels	coconut oil, hydrogenated vegetable oil, etc.)
milk products servings: 3 to 4 a day	ones which are low in saturated fat: skimmed milk and milk powder, low-fat products, buttermilk (from skim milk), low-fat yogurt, evaporated skim milk. low-fat or skim milk cheeses (without added cream): cottage cheese, farmer's, mozzarella, ricotta (from skim milk)	whole milk and whole milk products include: ice cream, cheeses made from whole milk or cream, butter; all creams (sour, half-and-half, whipped)
fats and oils (unsaturated types) servings: 5 to 8 teaspoons a day	margarine, liquid oil shortenings, salad dressings and mayonnaise made from polyunsaturated oils, vegetable oils; canola, corn, cottonseed, olive, sesame, partially hydrogenated soybean, sunflower, safflower	butter, lard, salt pork, meat fat, coconut oil, palm oil, palm kernel, completely hydrogenated margarine and shortenings; use peanut oil occasionally for flavor

Food Group	Acceptable	Avoid or Use Sparingly
sweets or desserts servings: no more than 2 servings a day	fruit ices, sherbet, gelatin, frozen yogurt, ice milk, fruit whip, angel food cake, low-fat commercially baked cakes, home-baked cookies and cake made with less fat and unsaturated fats, cocoa powder	coconut, cream products, fried food snacks (potato chips, corn chips, etc.), chocolate pudding, ice cream, and most commercial cakes, pies, cookies and mixes

Note: New, acceptable versions of standard products are appearing on the market. Be sure to read product labels carefully.

Serving Sizes

We are providing some general guidelines on serving sizes but please keep in mind that very young children will probably eat smaller portions and older kids will eat more. Serving size is far less important than making sure your youngster eats a variety of low-fat foods from each of the food groups. Because young children often eat only small amounts of food at one time, you may need to find creative ways to work everything in. Offer nutritious snacks—low-fat milk or fruit juice, cut up fruit, vegetable sticks, pasta salad, whole grain crackers and peanut butter, half a sandwich or half a cup of soup—between meals.

VEGETABLES: Figure on ½ cup per serving; more for raw leafy greens such as spinach or lettuce.

FRUITS: Figure on ½ cup or one small fruit per serving.

MILK PRODUCTS: Figure on 1 cup milk or yogurt or 1 ounce of cheese per serving.

BREADS AND CEREALS: Figure on 1 slice bread, ½ bagel, or ½ cup rice or pasta per serving.

WHAT YOU NEED TO KNOW ABOUT SATURATED FAT

We know that defatting the diet is the most important aspect of heart-healthy eating, but because there are different kinds of fats this can be somewhat confusing. Be especially diligent about cutting down on *saturated* fat, which is the type that naturally hardens at room temperature. Many experts believe that saturated fats are the main culprit in raising cholesterol levels, even more so than foods high in cholesterol. Here's a description of the basic types of fats.

SATURATED FAT: In reality, all fats are a mixture of saturated and unsaturated fatty acids. When a fat is mostly saturated, we refer to it as a saturated fat. Saturated fat comes mostly from animal foods, red meats, and whole milk dairy products. Processed foods made with tropical oils—palm oil, coconut oil, palm kernel oil—are also high in saturated fat. Popular kid foods—hot dogs, hamburgers, fried fast foods, snack cakes, cookies, and whole milk— are high in saturated fat.

MONOUNSATURATED FAT: These fats stay liquid at room temperature and help to lower the "bad" or LDL cholesterol without affecting the "good" or HDL cholesterol levels. Monounsaturated fats include olive oil and canola oil.

POLYUNSATURATED FAT: This category includes vegetable oils (not tropical oils) such as corn oil, safflower oil, and soybean oil. Unless the oil is hydrogenated (hydrogen is added to fat to harden it for use in processed foods and some margarine), this fat is liquid at room temperature. Polyunsaturates help to lower cholesterol levels, but some studies suggest that too much may pose other health risks.

Since poly- and monounsaturated fats don't raise cholesterol levels, shouldn't kids be able to eat unlimited amounts of them? Not really. The overall amount of fats in your child's diet is as important as the type of fat he or she eats. Research shows that a diet limited to 30 percent of calories from fat is best.

WHY YOUR CHILD NEEDS FIBER

Adding fiber to the diet, particularly water-soluble fiber, helps to keep cholesterol levels low. Good sources of soluble fiber include rice bran, oat bran, cornmeal, beans of all kinds, corn, citrus fruits, barley, unpeeled apples, peas, prunes, okra, and sweet potatoes.

While soluble fiber foods are good for cardiovascular health, insoluble fiber—found mainly in wheat bran—helps bowel regularity and may help reduce the risk of colon cancer. Both are important.

For foods rich in insoluble fiber, try whole wheat breads and crackers and whole wheat pasta. For soluble fiber make muffins using oat bran or rice bran. Shop for breads and cereals that contain oat bran or rice fiber. But read labels— many contain not only fiber but also high amounts of fat.

You've got it made if your youngster is willing to try a bowl of hot oatmeal. Although not as rich in soluble fiber as oat bran, the whole oat cereal offers a good dose of fiber, and some research shows that a bowlful of oatmeal is just as beneficial. It doesn't matter whether you buy instant, one minute cooking oats, or slow cooking oatmeal; the processing doesn't remove any of the fiber benefits. One caveat: if your child has high blood pressure and your pediatrician advises a salt watch, stay away from the instant kinds.

Some new high-fiber cereals have hit the market recently, aimed at the cholesterol-lowering consumer. The new cereals are made with psyllium (pronounced *silly-um*) which is a rich source of soluble fiber made from a grain grown in India. While eight times more potent than oat bran, psyllium-based products may not be appropriate for youngsters. Speak to your child's physician first.

Right now, researchers aren't sure just how much fiber is good for a youngster's diet. Too much can cause intestinal discomfort. The key is to introduce new items slowly, allowing your youngster's system to adapt a little at a time.

EATING OUT IS IN

We all love to eat out—kids and grown-ups alike. According to recent restaurant industry surveys, we eat more than 20 percent of our meals away from home in restaurants, cafeterias, pizza parlors, "submarine" sandwich shops, fast-food restaurants, and even convenience stores. Currently, fast food establishments account for four of every ten meals eaten out, and fast food tends to be low in fiber and high in calories, fat, and sodium.

We're busy people; we spend more than 40 percent of our food dollar and consume roughly a third of our calories and total fat eating out.

But to eat out heart-smart, you need to choose restaurants that prepare food well, and find out how the dish you select is prepared.

Try to choose items from the menu that are not fried and are made without cream or butter.

Below you will find some simple ways to be a dinner detective, but keep in mind that you also need to be assertive when ordering. For example, you can say, "My children enjoy pasta dishes, but we cannot have any made with butter or cream or high fat cheeses. What would you suggest?" If your server doesn't know, it's fine to request to see the restaurant manager.

Because it's easy to fill up on bread and butter or Chinese fried noodles even before you order, it's quite all right to refuse the butter or to request vegetables instead. Another good idea is to ask for soup to be served immediately while you and the kids are waiting for your dinner to be served. This is an especially good idea when you dine out with a youngster who is famished.

Your kids can help you find heart-healthy dishes by being dinner detectives. Even if they are not yet old enough to read the restaurant menu, you can discuss the dishes available and try to unravel the menu mysteries together.

Here are some clues:

- Key words to look for that indicate high-fat food include "butter" or "buttery"; "fried," "french fried," "deep fried," "batter fried," or "pan fried"; "breaded"; "creamed," "creamy," or "cream sauce"; "with gravy," "pan gravy," or "in its own gravy"; "hollandaise"; "au gratin" or "in cheese sauce"; "scalloped" or "escalloped"; "rich"; and "pastry."

- Terms that usually mean lower fat include "stir-fried," "roasted," "poached," and "steamed." Foods that are "grilled" or "broiled" can be lower fat if no fat is used during the preparation and fat is drained off during cooking.

Some terms are a little misleading. "Fresh" or "homemade" have nothing to do with low fat, and a product containing oat bran does not guarantee a healthful snack!

Fast food tends to be low in fiber and high in calories, fat, and sodium. If there is no alternative to a fast food restaurant, then:

- choose regular sandwiches instead of doubles, and plain types instead of those with lots of extras (bacon, sauces, etc.)

- avoid breaded, deep-fried fish or chicken sandwiches (especially those with cheese, tartar sauce, or mayonnaise)

- order roast beef for a leaner option than most burgers

- avoid fried chicken

- if your youngster insists on french fries, choose a small portion; better yet, look for places that serve baked potatoes

- at the salad bar, load up on fresh greens, fruits, and vegetables, but go easy on dressings and creamy salads; look for places that serve low-fat milk

- believe it or not, a plain hamburger on a bun with a slice of tomato is one of your best choices at fast food outlets.

Although it has 13 grams or 45 percent of its calories from fat, it's a lot better than chicken nuggets, which get 58 percent of the calories from fat, or some of the chicken sandwiches, which can have as much as 40 grams of fat *per serving*—the amount of fat you get in a pint and a half of ice cream!

SHOPPING

In the restaurant your children get to be dinner detectives. In the grocery store, enlist them as supermarket detectives! If you want to achieve a low-fat, low-cholesterol, high-fiber diet for your children—and by now I know that you do—you and your kids cannot just put into your shopping cart whatever looks appealing. First you have to read labels—and know how to interpret what you're reading!

How to Read Food Labels

All food labels list the product's ingredients in order of weight (the main ingredient is listed first, and the smallest ingredient is listed last). Stay away from items that list a fat or oil as one of the first four ingredients and avoid products that list several fats and oils in the ingredients.

Try to avoid products that contain these:

animal fat	hardened fat or oil
beef fat	hydrogenated vegetable oil
butter	lard
chicken fat	palm kernel oil
cocoa butter	turkey fat
coconut	vegetable oil*
coconut oil	vegetable shortening
cream	whole milk solids
egg and egg yolk solids	

*Could be coconut or palm oil.

Instead, choose products that do not contain fat or those that contain partially hydrogenated vegetable oils (cottonseed and/or soybean oil) or canola or olive oil.

Food manufacturers can give information on their labels in different ways. Providing an exact breakdown of cholesterol and fat content is optional, although new government laws are on the drawing board that would require food labels to tell us how much saturated fat, fiber, and percent of calories from fat we get in a serving. Serving sizes will be standardized, making it easier for us to compare products. Right now, however, manufacturers are allowed to use descriptive terms for cholesterol instead of giving quantities. To know what you're getting, you need to know how to translate the terms.

The Food and Drug Administration, which regulates most food products other than meat and poultry, currently allows manufacturers to label foods as follows:

- "cholesterol-free" means 2 milligrams of cholesterol or less per serving

- "low cholesterol" means 20 milligrams or less per serving

- "reduced cholesterol" means the cholesterol has been reduced by 75 percent or more; the cholesterol content of both the original item and the improved item must be shown

The U.S. Department of Agriculture, which regulates label claims for meat and poultry products, uses the following definitions:

- "extra lean" means no more than 5 percent fat by weight

- "lean" or "low fat" means no more than 10 percent fat by weight (be aware that "lean" does not necessarily mean less fat unless it is applied to meat)

- "light," "lite," "leaner," and "lower fat" all mean a reduction in fat of 25 percent or greater from comparable products

Many products today are labeled "low fat." The term "low fat" has legal meaning *only* when it is used to describe dairy products or meat. For milk, yogurt, or cheese to be labeled "low fat," the product must contain between 0.4 percent and 2 percent fat by weight.

Labels can be misleading. "No cholesterol" doesn't promise low fat, and "lite" doesn't necessarily mean the product is leaner. "Light" or "lite" on a label can refer to color, flavor, texture, or weight—not necessarily to calories. For example, "lite" olive oil is lighter in color and milder in flavor than regular olive oil, but the fat and calorie content is the same in both.

Figuring Fats in Food

On food labels, fat is listed in grams. If you know the number of grams of fat in a serving, and if you remember that 1 gram of fat has 9 calories, you can figure how many of the product's total calories come from fat. This is a useful thing to know. If the product is high in fat, you will know to avoid it or balance it with lower fat foods that day. No one meal will be right on the mark—you need to monitor your children's fat intake *throughout the day*.

To figure the percentage of calories from fat in a food:

1. Find the number of grams of fat per serving. (For example, 1 ounce of corn chips has 9 grams of fat.)

2. Multiply the number of grams of fat by 9, the number of calories in each gram. (One ounce of corn chips has 9×9 or 81 calories of fat.)

3. For a rough estimate, compare the number of calories from fat per serving to the total number of calories per serving. (One ounce of corn chips has 155 calories, of which 81 come from fat. You know right away that's more than half!)

4. For an exact percentage, divide the number of calories from fat per serving by the total number of calories per serving (in the corn chip example, 81 divided by 155 equals .52).

5. To read this figure as a percentage, multiply it by 100. (In our example, 52 percent of the calories in corn chips comes from fat.)

Two chocolate fudge sandwich cookies contain 7 grams of fat and have a total calorie count of 150 calories. When you do your fat figuring, you'll realize that there are 63 calories from fat in these cookies, and that fat accounts for 42 percent of the total number of calories. That's a lot! For about the same total calorie count, you can make a better choice—say, chocolate wafers. They have 2 grams of fat per 130 calories, which figures out to 13 percent.

Now let's take a walk through the supermarket, selecting low-fat items in each section. Once you've trained yourself and your kids how to do it, you'll find delicious low-fat foods in every department.

The Dairy Case

Milk

Remember, youngsters need at least 2 to 3 cups of milk a day, and the low-fat or skim-milk products are best. Check with your pediatrician regarding whether your children should be drinking skim, 1 percent, or 2 percent low-fat milk.

Funny as it sounds, buttermilk is a low-fat dairy food. Buttermilk is wonderful for adding low-fat calcium to baked goods, "creamed" soups, and salad dressings. So is canned evaporated skim milk. Avoid using evaporated whole milk or sweetened canned milks.

Look for nonfat milk powder cocoa mixes for a delicious cup of low-fat hot cocoa.

8 Ounces Milk	Fat (grams)
skim	1 (or less)
1 percent	2
2 percent	5
whole	8

Yogurt

When it comes to heart-smart yogurt, choose the brands made with skim milk or low-fat milk. Some children won't go for nonfat or low-fat yogurt but find it acceptable when blended in a salad dressing or added to baked goods.

8 Ounces Yogurt	Fat (grams)
plain, low-fat	4
flavored, low-fat	3
fruit, low-fat	2
fruit, whole milk	7

Cheese

While hard cheeses are very popular with children and an excellent source of calcium, they do contain high amounts of saturated fat. The good news is that there are plenty of reduced-fat choices. Try part skim mozarella, skim milk ricotta, or "lite" cream cheese. Look for cheeses that have 5 grams of fat or less per serving. Many brands of low-fat processed cheese or imitation cheese spreads are readily available at your supermarket. Be aware that some imitation cheeses replace butterfat with vegetable oil for a product that is lower in saturated fat, but whose overall fat content is still high. If your children insist on eating their usual kind of cheese, keep portion control in mind. A 1 ounce serving of cheese is the size of a 1 inch cube and contains a hefty amount of fat.

Reduced-fat Processed Cheeses	Fat (grams)
Borden Lite Line American (1½ slices)	2
Borden Lite Line Colby (1½ slices)	2
Borden Lite Line Sharp Cheddar (1½ slices)	2
Borden Lite Line Swiss (1½ slices)	2
Dorman's Light Mozzarella (1 ounce)	5
Polly-O Lite Mozzarella (1 ounce)	4
Weight Watchers American (1 slice)	2
Weight Watchers Shredded Cheddar (1 ounce)	5
Weight Watchers Swiss (1 slice)	2

Margarine

Choose margarine in which the first ingredient is liquid or try the ''reduced calorie'' brands (the first ingredient in diet margarine is usually water). Butter and margarine actually have the same amount of fat and calories, but the margarine has less saturated fat and is cholesterol free.

Eggs

According to recent findings by the USDA, eggs are not as high in cholesterol as was once believed, but you should still limit your child's intake to four egg yolks per week. Egg whites may be eaten freely.

The Meat Counter—Meat, Poultry, and Fish

Foods in the meat, poultry, and fish group are good sources of iron, zinc, vitamin B_6, and protein.

Heart-smart meat has the fat trimmed off; poultry should be served without the skin. Choose sausages and hot dogs made from chicken or turkey—many contain one-third less fat. You do not need to eat these foods every day, but when you choose to eat them, here are some heart-smart choices.

- *Beef:* Choose round, loin, flank, chuck (arm) steaks, or roasts, especially ''select'' grade cuts. Shop for meats that are labeled ''choice'' rather than for pieces that are well-marbled with fat.

- *Pork:* Select tenderloin, center loin roast.

- *Veal:* Choose lean cuts, such as scallopine, round.

- *Frankfurters and sausages:* Select chicken or turkey products only.

- *Lamb:* Choose leg, loin roasts.

- *Chicken and turkey:* Select breast parts and serve them skinless.

• *Fish and shellfish:* All types are acceptable. They are high in omega-3 fatty acids, which may help prevent heart disease. Fatty fish such as salmon are acceptable because they are high in omega-3. Tuna and other fish caught in cold waters are also good choices.

Ground Beef

Available in many different forms, ground beef accounts for about 25 percent of our fat intake. Although there is considerable variation from store to store, *ground beef* is usually higher in fat than *ground chuck,* while *ground round* and *ground sirloin* are leaner. Fat content ranges from about 16 to 28 percent by weight. Some supermarkets label ground beef as regular, lean, and extra lean.

Ground Turkey

Although ground turkey is leaner than other ground meats, many brands may not be as lean as you think. Because there are no government standards for the amount of fat in ground turkey, the fat content may vary from brand to brand. Some brands contain mostly dark meat, which is higher in fat than white meat. Some brands grind in the skin and fat. If you want superlean ground turkey, buy skinned, boneless turkey breast and ask the butcher to grind it or grind it yourself. This way is a little more expensive and more troublesome, but you are assured of getting a product with fewer than 2 grams of fat per 3 ounce serving.

If you prefer to buy turkey that is already ground, look for products with nutrition information on the label. Some good choices with fewer than 6 grams of fat per 3 ounce serving include Perdue ground turkey, Shady Brook Farms ground turkey, and The Turkey Store ground turkey. Even though these items may be higher in fat than the "grind your own," you're still way ahead when compared to ground beef. Even the leanest type of beef contains 14 grams of fat in a 3 ounce portion.

Cold Cuts

More meat companies are cutting the fat from cold cuts. Oscar Mayer with "Our Leanest Cuts"; Hillshire Farms

"Deli Select" pastrami, smoked turkey, and Cajun ham; and Butterball, with its turkey ham and turkey salami are among the manufacturers looking to woo the fat-conscious consumer. That's the good part.

The tricky part is getting past their label claims—"95 percent fat free" or "86 percent fat free." This sounds great, but it is only part of the story. These figures indicate the percentage of fat by *weight*. As we've seen, a fat watcher needs to know the percentage of fat by *calories*. They're not the same. A cold cut that is 95 percent fat free might still derive 45 percent of its calories from fat. The new labeling laws will require manufacturers to use the same portion size and to provide the percentage of calories from fat. This will make it much easier to compare products.

To make heart-smart choices at the deli counter, go for products that have 3 grams of fat or less per serving. And be wary of other tricky label claims; the product that says it has only 30 calories per slice sounds good, but if you need three of these paper-thin slices to equal a serving, you may end up with exactly the same fat content per serving as other brands.

Breads

In recent years, supermarkets have added bakeries offering a variety of bread products and sweet baked breads. Baked goods vary widely in fat content. Muffins—even the ones made with oat bran—are higher in fat than, for example, dinner rolls, English muffins, or bagels. Croissants and biscuits are higher in fat than most other bread and rolls. Pita breads, English muffins, and tortillas are low in fat and good bread choices. Some brands of pita and English muffins are made with whole wheat flour for a double dose of health benefits.

In general, whole grain breads are best. Bread manufacturers offer a large variety of whole grain breads, some made with oat bran, rice bran, bulgur wheat, or even triticale. Have your youngster sample these fiber-rich breads.

Cereals

Most cold cereals are low in fat, with the exception of the granola cereals. Read those labels!

Breakfast cereals can be a good source of fiber. Whole grain cereals such as shredded wheat, bran flakes, or oatmeal provide more fiber than corn or rice cereals. One ounce of bran flakes contains over 4 grams of fiber, 1 ounce of shredded wheat has almost 3 grams of fiber, and 1 ounce of rice crinkles has less than ½ gram of fiber.

Children do not need cereals that are superrich in fiber. Choose cereals that contain 2 to 5 grams of fiber per serving. And while you're checking the fat and fiber content, take a look at the sugar content, which is listed on the side of the box in grams per serving. Select cereals with no more than 5 to 8 grams of sugar per serving.

Fruits and Vegetables

Nearly every item in the produce section is a heart-smart food. When it comes to choosing fruits and vegetables, aim for variety. Remember, to lower our fat intake, we need to fill up on the good-for-you leafy greens, carotene-rich melons, and potassium-rich oranges. For convenience, check out the salad bar in your market.

When buying salad greens, go for color. Dark green and leafy romaine, escarole, watercress, spinach, parsley, and broccoli are much better sources of vitamins and minerals than plain old iceberg lettuce. But dark green and leafy vegetables are sharper in taste and rejected by many youngsters. Try mixing the two together, a little bit of romaine with a few leaves of iceberg lettuce for starters.

For good sources of vitamin A, look for items that are orange or deep yellow. Kids love carrots, and most are pleased with cantaloupe. Pumpkin is another good source, and there's a wonderful heart-smart Pumpkin Muffin, made conveniently with canned pumpkin puree (see page 45). Baked sweet potatoes topped with a little cinnamon-spiked applesauce make a wonderful cold weather after-school snack.

For vitamin C, choose oranges, tangerines, red and green peppers, and strawberries.

For potassium and fiber, go for bananas. Use them as snacks, to sweeten cereals, in milk shakes, or in baked goods.

Snacks and Crackers

This category is probably the toughest one in which to make heart-smart selections. Many commercial snacks are far too high in sugar, preservatives, and artificial food color. Most offer too many "empty" calories—few nutrients for the calories they provide.

But kids love snacks, especially the sweet, crunchy, salty, fatty kind. And snacks are an important source of calories for many growing children. So all we can hope to do is select the healthiest snack in each category and limit the portion size.

Here are some guidelines:

- Avoid packages that contain butter, lard, coconut oil, palm or palm kernal oil and completely hydrogenated margarine and shortenings. If the label is inexact—for example, "palm or soybean oil"—assume the worst.

- Crackers vary widely in fat content. Crackers that feel greasy to the touch are high in fat. Heart-smart cracker choices include rice cakes, matzoh, melba toast, whole wheat wafers, and saltines. The new rice cracker mixes are low in fat but unacceptably high in sodium.

- Good low-fat crunchy snacks include pretzels, plain popcorn, unsalted soda crackers, and sesame-topped bread sticks. But beware; even after you've selected a heart-smart snack, you still need to read food labels. Some microwave varieties of popcorn and even some "air popped" brands have more fat than potato chips!

- Dried fruits can be eaten in moderation. Avoid banana chips which contain too much added sugar.

• Heart-smart cookies choices include gingersnaps, vanilla wafers, graham crackers, oatmeal cookies, raisin bars, and fig bars. As you'll see from the following chart, some cookies have *six times as much fat* as others.

Brand	Cookies (per 1 ounce serving)	Calories	Fat (grams)	Percent of Calories from Fat
Archway				
Date-filled Oatmeal	1	90	1	10
Molasses	1	100	2	18
Health Valley				
Amaranth	2	140	6	39
Fruit Jumbos Almond Date	2	140	6	39
Keebler				
Pecan Sandies	2	160	10	56
Cinnamon Crisp Graham	8*	140	4	26
Old-Fashioned Oatmeal	2	160	6	34
E.L. Fudge Sandwich	2	140	6	38
Nabisco				
Lorna Doone shortbread	4	140	7	45
Chips Ahoy	3	140	7	45
Fig Newtons	2	100	2	18
Oreos	3	140	6	39
Old-Fashioned Gingersnaps	4	120	3	23
Vanilla Wafers	7	130	4	28
Honey Maid				
Cinnamon or Raisin Graham	8*	120	2	15

Brand	Cookies (per 1 ounce serving)	Calories	Fat (grams)	Percent of Calories from Fat
Peek Freans				
Arrowroot	3	130	4	28
Fruit Creme	2	140	6	39
Ginger Crisp	3	130	3	21
Shortcake	2	145	7	43
Pepperidge Farm				
Lido	2	180	11	55
Brussels Mint	3	200	10	45
Gingerman	4	130	5	35
Molasses Crisps	5	165	8	44
Almond Supreme	2	140	10	64
Sunshine				
Hydrox	3	160	7	40
Golden Fruit Raisin Biscuit	2	150	3	18
Cinnamon Graham	8*	140	6	39
Chip-A-Roos	2	130	7	48
Honey Graham	8*	120	4	30

*Sections

Chart reprinted with permission of *University of California, Berkeley Wellness Letter.*

As your family gets used to your healthier way of eating, substitution is the name of the game. Instead of potato chips or peanuts, offer pretzels or low-fat popcorn. Instead of pepperoni pizza, try pizza with lots of vegetables. Instead of ice cream, go for frozen yogurt or ice milk—with chocolate syrup on top instead of hot fudge. A half cup of frozen yogurt has 2 grams of fat, an equal serving of ice cream has 5 grams of fat—even more in the premium brands. Frozen dietary desserts such as American Glacé and Vitari are also good low-fat choices. If your children feel deprived without candy, offer them plain M & M's, Gummy Bears, lollipops, and jelly beans instead of gooey chocolate bars and cream-filled candies. You may not be cutting back much on the sugar, but you will be making progress in the fat department.

FINDING HIDDEN FATS IN FOODS

You'll probably be surprised to see how much fat is contained in these common foods.

	Teaspoons of Fat*
1 raised doughnut	2
1/2 cup granola	2
1/2 cup "gourmet" ice cream	4
2 slices or 1½ ounces bologna	3
1 small hot dog	3
5 snack crackers	1
3 chocolate chip cookies	2
1 slice apple pie	2
1 ounce potato chips	2

*One teaspoon of fat equals 5 grams.
SOURCE: Nutritive Value of Convenience and Processed Foods, © 1986 The American Dietetic Association.

COOKING HEART-SMART

When my daughters were growing up, the first question they asked when they came home from school was "What's for dinner?" The answer was usually, "hamburgers" or "franks" or "pot roast" or "stew" or "meatloaf" or "meatballs and spaghetti"—all heavy, meat-based meals.

My grandchildren will ask the same questions someday, but I'm sure my daughters will have new answers: "pasta and vegetables with meat sauce," "vegetable lasagna," "turkey loaf," "thick bean soup with small chunks of ham."

The difference will be in the focus—lots of vegetables, grains, and beans and small amounts of animal protein—as well as the preparation. The easiest way to immediately cut back on your family's fat intake is to limit the fat you add to food—the butter on the potato, cream in the soup, etc.

My grandchildren will have more of their foods grilled and broiled, and foods will be fried only once in a while.

Here are more heart-smart cooking tips.

1. When cooking meat or poultry, trim all visible fat. Remove the skin from poultry before serving. Buy tuna or other fish packed in water, or if you buy it in oil rinse it in a strainer before adding it to a salad or casserole.

2. Broil, roast, poach, grill, steam, and bake rather than fry. When you roast, place the meat on a rack so that fat can drip away, and baste with fat-free ingredients such as wine, tomato juice, or lemon juice. Forget self-basting turkeys; many have coconut oil—high in saturated fat!

3. To cut the fat from soups and stews, make them in advance, refrigerate, and skim the fat that forms on the top before reheating.

4. Ground meat can almost always be browned without adding extra fat, even when a nonstick skillet is not available. Simply begin cooking over medium heat until the meat releases some fat; then raise the heat to medium high.

5. Use nonstick skillets because then less fat is required for cooking. Shop for nonstick vegetable sprays.

6. To cut fat in salad dressings, make your own using low-fat yogurt, buttermilk, and flavored vinegars. Cut way down on the classic proportion of three parts oil to one part vinegar. Try a mixture of half oil and half vinegar, or use even less oil when adding low-fat buttermilk or yogurt.

7. Use reduced-calorie mayonnaise, margarine, and salad dressings. You cut the fat by 30 percent.

8. Use unsweetened plain cocoa powder instead of baking chocolate whenever possible. Cocoa powder provides the same rich taste as chocolate but has far less fat because most of the cocoa butter has been removed. Instead of 1 ounce of baking chocolate, use 3 tablespoons of cocoa plus 1 tablespoon of vegetable oil.

9. When making cakes or soft drop cookies, use no more than 2 to 3 tablespoons fat per cup of flour.

10. For muffins, quick breads, and biscuits, limit fat to 1 to 2 tablespoons per cup of flour.

HEART-SMART SUBSTITUTIONS

Instead of	Use
1 tablespoon butter	1 tablespoon margarine
1 cup shortening	2/3 cup vegetable oil*
1 whole egg	2 egg whites
1 cup whole milk	1 cup skim milk
light cream	Equal portion 1 percent milk and evaporated skim milk
sour cream	Blend 1 cup low-fat cottage cheese with 1 tablespoon skim milk and 2 tablespoons lemon juice, or use low-fat plain yogurt with a small amount of mayonnaise mixed in. Choose fat-reduced mayonnaise—most youngsters won't notice any difference.

*Canola oil and olive oil are heart-smart choices. Use canola oil in recipes and olive oil in salad dressings.

USING THE MENU PLANS

Okay, so now you know why a heart-smart diet is important for children and for the whole family. You know how to shop and how to start cooking the low-fat way, and we've shown you how minor changes and substitutions can go far in reducing the fat content of your children's meals.

Now to make your life even easier, we offer five complete menus using recipes from the book. Each daily menu contains no more than 30 percent total fat, with no more than 10 percent of the fat from saturated fat. On average, the menus supply around 2000 calories per day. Please remember that calorie requirements vary widely, depending on a youngster's age, weight, activity level, etc. If you don't know how many calories your child needs per day, consult his or her doctor.

You may want to follow the daily guide exactly, or you may want to pick and choose what you think your family will like. Each recipe includes a nutritional analysis which tells you just how many calories, total grams of fat and saturated fat, and milligrams of cholesterol the finished recipe contains. We also tell you what percentage of calories in the recipe comes from fat. This information will help you when you make your own menu plans using the recipes in the book.

Menu 1

BREAKFAST
Orange Juice
Kim's Raisin Bread Pudding (p. 41)
Jen's Nonfat Cocoa (1 cup) (p. 46)

LUNCH
Pita Fajitta (p. 50)
Apple
Cheesy Pretzel (1) (p. 106)
Low-Fat Milk* (8 ounces)

SNACK
Matthew's Favorite Soup (p. 57)
Italian Bread and Margarine (2 teaspoons)

DINNER
Mixed Fruit Cup (½ cup)
"Oven-Fried" Fish (p. 64)
Mashed Potatoes (p. 66)
2 Cups Tossed Salad and Italian Salad Dressing
    (2 tablespoons)
Slice Whole Wheat Bread and Margarine (2 teaspoons)
Steamed Broccoli (1 cup)
Chocolate Pudding (p. 81)
Low-Fat Milk* (8 ounces)

Total Calories: 2227
Total Fat: 25 percent
Saturated Fat: 7 percent
Cholesterol: 228 milligrams

*1 percent milkfat

Menu 2

BREAKFAST
Cantaloupe Slices (½ cup)
Cheese and Apple Pizza (p. 44)
Low-Fat Milk* (8 ounces)

LUNCH
Peanut Butter (2 tablespoons) and Shredded Carrots
    in Pita Pouch
Low-Fat Milk* (8 ounces)
Tangerine
Banana Snack Cake (p. 87)

SNACK
Platter of Cut-Up Raw Veggies (2 cups)
Spinach Dip (p. 98)

DINNER
Heart-Smart Hamburger on a Bun (p. 78)
Tossed Salad with Tomato Slices and Alfalfa Sprouts and
    French Salad Dressing (1 tablespoon)
Vegetarian Baked Beans (½ cup)
Natural Soda—Half Seltzer, Half Grape Juice
Chips 'n' Oats Cookie (1) (p. 91)
Low-Fat Milk* (8 ounces)

Total Calories: 2094
Total Fat: 28 percent
Saturated Fat: 6 percent
Cholesterol: 145 milligrams

*1 percent milkfat

Menu 3

BREAKFAST
Fresh Strawberries (½ cup)
Laurie's Pancakes (2) (p. 40)
Low-Fat Milk* (8 ounces)
Pancake Syrup (1 tablespoon)

LUNCH
Roast Beef and Coleslaw in Pita Pouch (p. 51)
Carrot Sticks, Green Pepper Slices
Low-Fat Milk* (8 ounces)
Small Bunch Grapes (1 cup)

SNACK
Oven-Baked French Fries (p. 97)
Natural Soda—Half Grape Juice, Half Seltzer

DINNER
Sweet and Sour Turkey Meatballs (p. 77)
Macaroni (½ cup)
Zucchini Spears, Broccoli Florettes, and Salad Dressing
    (1 tablespoon) for Dipping
Italian Bread and Margarine (1 teaspoon)
Banana Split (p. 83)

Total Calories: 1979
Total Fat: 24 percent
Saturated Fat: 5 percent
Cholesterol: 200 milligrams

*1 percent milkfat

Menu 4

BREAKFAST
Orange Juice (½ cup)
Ed's Omelette (p. 42)
Whole Wheat Toast and Margarine (1 teaspoon)
Low-Fat Milk* (8 ounces)

LUNCH
Manhattan Clam Chowder (p. 58)
Tuna Fish Sandwich on Rye Bread (3 ounces)
Cherry Tomatoes, Carrot Sticks
Pineapple Juice (6 ounces)

SNACK
Apple-Raspberry Chill (p. 100)
Cheesy Pretzels (2) (p. 106)

DINNER
Tamale Pie (p. 72)
Tossed Salad (2 cups) with French Salad Dressing
    (1 tablespoon)
Bread Sticks (4 small)
Low-Fat Milk* (8 ounces)
Fruit Kebobs with Creamy Dip (p. 85)

Total Calories: 1765
Total Fat: 30 percent
Saturated Fat: 6 percent
Cholesterol: 233 milligrams

*1 percent milkfat

Menu 5

BREAKFAST
Orange Wedges (1 orange)
Pumpkin Muffin (p. 45)
Low-Fat Vanilla Yogurt (1 cup)

LUNCH
Hurry-Up Soup (p. 54)
Turkey Sandwich (3½ ounces white meat) with Lettuce and
    Tomato with Mayonnaise (1 tablespoon)
Carrot Sticks
Apple Juice (6 ounces)

SNACK
Fresh Fruit Sipper (p. 100)

DINNER
Beef and Broccoli Stir-Fry (p. 68)
Brown Rice (1 cup)
Tossed Salad (2 cups) with Salad Dressing (1 tablespoon)
Blueberry Cobbler (p. 82)
Low-Fat Milk* (8 ounces)

Total Calories: 2110
Total Fat: 28 percent
Saturated Fat: 6 percent
Cholesterol: 173 milligrams

*1 percent milkfat

The Recipes

Abbreviations and Symbols

gm:	gram
mg:	milligram
sat.:	saturated

BREAKFAST

Studies show that youngsters who eat breakfast do better in school. They are more alert and have more concentration throughout the morning. One recent study of 530 school-age youngsters who ate a ready-to-eat cereal for breakfast showed the youngsters had blood cholesterol levels 8 percent lower than students consuming a noncereal breakfast and 12 percent lower than those students who skipped breakfast. The most desirable cholesterol levels were found among students who consumed a ready-to-eat cereal containing 2 grams of fiber per serving (more fiber was not offered).

The reason? These findings suggest that breakfast habits are a good marker of a heart-healthy life-style, according to the researchers who presented their study at a meeting of the American Dietetic Association. Children who skipped breakfast had the most unfavorable body weights, were less knowledgeable about nutrition, and were least likely to make healthy snack choices.

A well-balanced morning meal should include:

- a serving of a protein-rich food—low-fat milk or yogurt, low-fat cheese, fish or skinless poultry, or peanut butter (in moderation, please!)

- a vitamin C-rich food such as an orange, grapefruit slices, strawberries, cantaloupe

- a food rich in complex carbohydrates—whole grain cereal, bread, muffin

- a small dab of fat—a little margarine or vegetable oil

An orange cut in quarters, a slice of whole wheat toast with a bowl of unsweetened cereal splashed with low-fat milk is just fine. And fast. But in many households, even this takes up too much time. Simple changes can help. You might want to set the table the night before, cut up the orange and leave it in the refrigerator.

Your next best bet is to send along a snack to eat on the way out the door or at a scheduled snack time in school. Peanut butter and crackers is a good "send along." So is the nutrient-studded pumpkin muffin to have with a container of low-fat milk at snack time. (See recipe page 45).

If eggs are a popular breakfast mainstay, better to poach, boil, or fry them in a nonstick pan without fat—and remember that 4 egg yolks per week is the recommended limit. To cut cholesterol use 1 yolk with 2 egg whites. This works fine when making French toast or even omelettes.

And what if your family won't give up their morning meats? A 3-inch sausage patty can have as much as 17 grams of fat and just three slices of bacon contain 9 grams, most of which is saturated. A better choice would be Canadian bacon—which contains 4 grams of fat in two slices. Even better, try our recipe for heart-smart sausage patties with only 1½ grams of fat per patty.

Sifting through the cereal aisle for what's best to buy the kids can be a tedious chore. Most cereals are low in fat and cholesterol free, but you'll want to limit the amounts of sugar and make sure that the cereal contains enough fiber.

Here are some "cereal bowl" guidelines:

- *Fiber*: look for cereals with about 2 to 3 grams per serving for younger children; older children can have 5 grams per serving

- *Sugar*: less than 5 grams of sugar per *dry* serving (that's about 1 teaspoon of sugar)

- *Sodium*: no more than 300 milligrams per serving (before milk is added)

- *Fat*: 2 grams or less per serving

Here are some brand name cereals that come close to meeting our guidelines, yet tasty enough to please the kids:

New Morning Oatios
Post's Raisin Bran
New Morning Fruit-E-O's
Kellogg's Apple Cinnamon Squares
General Mills Cheerios
General Mills Oatmeal Raisin Crisp
Quaker Oats Corn Cereal

Basic Pancake Mix

Children adore pancakes. Make a large dry mix in advance and then simply blend the mix with liquid ingredients for a quick breakfast. Here's the mix, updated to include a combination of rice bran and oat bran for a boost of soluble fiber. Because the mix includes nonfat dry milk, the pancakes are a good source of calcium.

Makes 12 cups

1	cup oat bran
1	cup rice bran
8	cups unbleached flour
1⅔	cups nonfat dry milk
⅓	cup baking powder
2½	teaspoons salt
1	cup canola oil

1. In a large container (6 to 8 quarts capacity), thoroughly mix both brans, flour, dry milk, baking powder, and salt.
2. Add oil and blend well, using a wooden spoon or your hands.
3. Store tightly in the refrigerator. Lasts about 3 weeks.

Preparation time: 15 minutes
Nutrients per serving:

Calories: 128	Sat. fat: less than 1 gm
Total fat: 5 gm	Cholesterol: less than 1 mg

Percentage of calories from fat: 34

Laurie's Pancakes

Let your youngster help make the batter. Even a four year old will love pitching in. For a special treat, try making star-shaped or animal-shaped pancakes. Young children will be thrilled!

Makes 12 pancakes

2 cups basic pancake mix
1 tablespoon sugar
1 egg, slightly beaten
1 cup water

1. Stir pancake mix and sugar together.
2. Mix egg and water thoroughly. Add to pancake mix and sugar. Stir until dry ingredients are barely moistened. Batter will be lumpy.
3. For each pancake, pour batter onto a nonstick or slightly oiled hot griddle or fry pan, using about 2 tablespoons batter per pancake. Cook until top is bubbly and edges begin to set. Turn and cook the other side.

Preparation time: 5 minutes
Cooking time: about 15 minutes
Nutrients per 2 pancakes:
   Calories: 190   Sat. fat: less than 2 gm
   Total fat: 7 gm   Cholesterol: 36 mg
          Percentage of calories from fat: 34

Kim's Raisin Bread Pudding

My youngest daughter, Kimberly, was the quintessential sleepyhead—even a moment to down a glass of OJ would cause a preschool squabble. Everything changed when she tasted my raisin bread pudding, a fine morning fuel food. The egg offers protein, there's some calcium from the milk, and carbohydrates from the bread. Prepare the night before and refrigerate.

Makes 4 servings

1½ cups (about 4 slices) raisin bread cut into cubes
¼ cup raisins
2 tablespoons sugar
¾ teaspoon ground cinnamon
1 egg
¼ teaspoon vanilla
1¼ cups skim milk

1. Preheat oven to 325° F. Spray a 1 quart baking casserole with nonstick vegetable spray. Put bread cubes into casserole and sprinkle with raisins.

2. In a separate bowl, mix sugar and cinnamon and stir in egg; add vanilla.

3. Heat milk and slowly stir into egg mixture and pour over bread. Bake for 40 minutes or until tester when inserted into the pudding comes out clean. Can be made in advance, refrigerated, and reheated.

Preparation time: 15 minutes
Cooking time: 40 minutes
Nutrients per serving:
  Calories: 164   Sat. fat: less than 1 gm
  Total fat: 2 gm   Cholesterol: 55 mg
          Percentage of calories from fat: 11

Ed's Omelette

Omelettes can be part of a heart-healthy breakfast when some of the yolk is eliminated. Here's a delicious omelette my husband developed when we learned our daughter Laurie had a high cholesterol reading. (P.S. She never noticed a change!)

Makes 3 servings

      Nonstick vegetable spray
 1   whole egg
 3   egg whites
 1   tablespoon water
 ⅓   cup reduced-calorie shredded cheddar cheese

1. Coat skillet with spray and place over medium heat. In a bowl, using a fork, beat eggs well, blending with water.

2. Pour mixture into heated skillet and gently rotate skillet so egg mixture covers entire surface.

3. Sprinkle cheese over eggs and as cheese begins to melt and eggs begin to set, fold omelette envelope-style and continue cooking until desired doneness.

Preparation time: 5 minutes
Cooking time: 10 minutes
Nutrients per serving:
    Calories: 84   Sat. fat: 2 gm
    Total fat: 4 gm   Cholesterol: 80 mg
              Percentage of calories from fat: 48

Michael's Turkey Breakfast Sausage

Here's a "make ahead" recipe for lean sausage patties. The secret is low-fat turkey instead of pork, blended with fiber-rich oats. Trust us, your kids won't know the difference.

Makes 32 patties
(two patties per serving)

1	cup quick cooking (not instant) oats
3	6-ounce cans tomato juice
1	pound ground turkey (white meat)
1¼	teaspoons ground sage
¾	teaspoon salt
1	teaspoon freshly ground black pepper
½	teaspoon ground ginger
¼	teaspoon dried thyme leaves

1. In a large bowl, soak oats in tomato juice for about 15 minutes. Add turkey, sage, salt and pepper, ginger, and thyme. Mix with your hands or wooden spoon until well blended. (Mixture will be sticky.)

2. Place mixture on plastic wrap and form into a 12-inch-long log. Wrap and freeze until firm enough to slice, about 1½ to 2 hours. Do not freeze solid.

3. Remove from freezer and unwrap. Cut patties into 32 slices, each about ⅜ inch thick.

4. Wrap patties in squares of aluminum foil, two to four patties per square. Place in an airtight container and return to freezer. (Patties can be frozen up to one month.)

5. When ready to serve, remove patties as needed from freezer and pan fry in a lightly sprayed nonstick skillet over medium heat, turning once, about 8 to 10 minutes, or until no longer pink inside.

Preparation time: 20 minutes (plus freezing time)
Cooking time: 10 minutes
Nutrients per serving:

Calories: 68	Sat. fat: 1 gm
Total fat: 3 gm	Cholesterol: 19 mg

Percentage of calories from fat: 41

Cheese and Apple Pizza

Here's a recipe that sounds a bit offbeat but our pint-size sampler, Joe, loved it. He giggled when we told him he was eating pizza for breakfast.

Makes 4 servings

2   7-inch whole wheat pita breads
½   cup part skim ricotta cheese
2   teaspoons reduced calorie margarine
1   teaspoon brown sugar
½   cup orange juice
½   teaspoon cinnamon
1   large apple, cored and sliced thin

1. Preheat oven to 350° F. Split pita bread in half horizontally.

2. Place pitas on cookie sheet and bake until slightly toasted, about 5 minutes.

3. Remove pitas from oven and place on serving plates. Divide ricotta cheese and spoon equally onto the 4 bread halves.

4. Meantime, melt margarine in skillet. Add sugar, juice, cinnamon, and apple slices. Cook over medium-high heat for about 5 minutes, stirring occasionally, or until apples soften and sauce thickens slightly.

5. Fan apple slices on ricotta cheese, then spoon liquid evenly over apple slices.

Preparation time: 10 minutes
Cooking time: 10 minutes
Nutrients per serving:
  Calories: 179   Sat. fat: 2 gm
  Total fat: 4 gm   Cholesterol: 9 mg
            Percentage of calories from fat: 19

Pumpkin Muffins

Pumpkin puree gives these pumpkin muffins their moistness and good color—that's the part the kids should like. And Mom and Dad should like the muffin for its powerhouse of wonderful nutrients—a nice breakfast "send-along."

Makes 24 muffins

2½   cups all-purpose flour
¾   cup sugar
2   tablespoons baking powder
2   teaspoons ground cinnamon
¼   teaspoon salt
2   eggs plus 2 egg whites, slightly beaten
1   cup skim milk
½   cup canola oil
1   cup canned pumpkin
1   tablespoon vanilla
1   cup chopped golden raisins
½   cup chopped walnuts, optional

1. Preheat oven to 350° F. Place 24 paper baking cups in muffin tins.

2. Mix together thoroughly flour, sugar, baking powder, cinnamon, and salt.

3. In another bowl, mix eggs, skim milk, oil, pumpkin, and vanilla; add to dry ingredients and stir until barely moistened. Fold in raisins and walnuts.

4. Fill paper cup two thirds full. Bake 20 minutes or until toothpick inserted in center comes out clean.

6. Remove from muffin tins and cool on rack.

Note: For later use, wrap muffins in aluminum foil and store in freezer. When ready to use, unwrap and defrost. Reheat in toaster oven.

Preparation time: 25 minutes
Baking time: about 20 minutes
Nutrients per serving:
   Calories: 147   Sat. fat: less than 1 gm
   Total fat: 5 gm   Cholesterol: 18 mg
        Percentage of calories from fat: 31

Jen's Nonfat Cocoa Mix

Here's a delicious low-fat hot drink that offers a wallop of calcium needed by growing children. Have your youngster help prepare the mix in advance. A good hands-on project if they are struggling with fractions.

Makes 6 cups

4   cups nonfat dry milk
¾   cup unsweetened cocoa
1¼ cups sugar

1. Combine dry milk, cocoa, and sugar in a large container with a lip. Stir well.
2. Store, tightly covered, in a cool dry place.
3. When ready to serve, stir mixture and for each one cup serving place 3½ tablespoons of mixture into a cup, and slowly add boiling water, a little at a time, stirring as you pour.

Preparation time: 10 minutes
Cooking time: none
Nutrients per serving:
  Calories: 78   Sat. fat: less than 1 gm
  Total fat: less than   Cholesterol: 2 mg
    1 gm
          Percentage of calories from fat: 6

LUNCH

Packing a nutritious brown-bag lunch is no guarantee that junior will gobble it up. There's so much going on at lunchtime; playing baseball or jump rope may have more appeal than eating a boring meal. To maximize the chance your kid will actually eat what is in his lunch pail, offer foods with kid appeal. Here are some suggestions:

- Let your youngster help decide the lunch pail menu.

- Try adding foods with varied shapes, colors, textures. Sandwich fillings are best kept simple, but you can add interest by changing breads or cutting sandwiches in different ways. Try roast beef in a pita pouch; use a heart-shaped cookie cuter to shape a peanut butter sandwich. (Keep a supply of cookie cutters on hand—car, heart, flower.)

- Surprise your child with a hot food favorite. Leftover macaroni and cheese (see p. 69), pasta and meatballs, or his or her favorite soup. Pack hot food in a thermal bottle according to instructions to insure safety.

- Include fresh vegetable sticks and/or fresh fruit. Fruit can be cut into bite-sized pieces for younger children (dip in lemon juice to prevent browning), or packed whole.

- Desserts or snacks can be a homemade nutritious cookie, cake, or muffin, or a lower fat, store-bought item such as graham crackers, gingersnaps, vanilla wafers, fig bars, or unsalted pretzels.

- Most schools offer lower fat milk. If not, send along a small container—but make sure it will stay chilled. Other choices can include containers of fruit juice. Avoid fruit drinks, punches, and sodas which contain large amounts of sugar but varying levels of juice and nutrients.

- It's okay now and then to include your child's favorite treat even if it's high in sugar, fat, or salt—say, a small bag of potato chips or small candy bar. Balance this choice with other healthy and low-fat foods throughout the day.

- Send a love note. Remind your youngster how good he must feel about his or her *A* on a math test, the way he cleaned his room, the home run he had in the ball game, etc.

- If your child likes to trade at lunchtime, include a special "trading" treat—maybe an extra homemade cookie, a small bag of pretzels, a small cluster of grapes.

A good lunch includes at least one serving of a fruit or vegetable. Here are some suggestions with "kid appeal."

Vegetables	*Fruits*
cucumber spears	apricots
broccoli florets	cherries
cherry tomatoes	grapes
green pepper strips	melon wedges
carrot sticks	nectarine
zucchini sticks	banana
snowpeas	tangerine
celery	peach
	plum

SANDWICHES

Simple Sandwich Suggestions

- Layer part skim mozzarella cheese and sliced turkey breast on rye bread spread with apple butter and shredded lettuce.

- Slice cooked egg whites and layer with sliced tomato and shredded lettuce and pack in pita pouch.

- Try lean boiled ham with a little pickle relish.

- Try water-packed tuna fish mixed with reduced-calorie mayonnaise and lots of diced celery.

- Try leftover white meat chicken layered with red pepper strips or pimentos for older kids.

- Turkey-based cold cuts are popular kid-type sandwiches. While turkey based products are much lower in fat, they are high in sodium. Although not all children need to be mindful of a sodium intake, it's best to use these products now and then and vary the sandwich fillings.

- Peanut butter *again??* For those youngsters who want peanut butter or nothing, consider adding some variety to the same old sandwich filling. Try peanut butter and sliced banana, peanut butter and shredded carrots, peanut butter and raisins, peanut butter and sliced strawberries, peanut butter and sliced apple.

Note: While peanut butter is high in overall fat, it contains a good amount of monounsaturated fat (the "good" kind) and an acceptable amount of saturated fat (the kind you're supposed to avoid). And since it is cholesterol free and rich in vitamins and minerals, overall, peanut butter is a perfectly fine sandwich filling when used in moderation.

For brown bagging it safely:

- Pack already-chilled foods in an insulated lunch box, bag, or cooler.

- If packing soup, make sure liquid is not too hot.

- Freeze sandwich the night before. It will thaw by lunch-time and keep the rest of the lunch pail cool too.

- For best quality, don't freeze sandwiches with mayonnaise, salad dressing, or hard-cooked eggs.

Pita Fajitta

If you're grilling chicken breasts for dinner some night, make a few extra to use as a lunchtime "send along." Here's a sandwich idea for older children with heartier appetites.

Makes 2 sandwiches

6	ounces chicken breast, skin removed
	Chili powder, cumin, pepper, and salt to taste
½	tomato, chopped
½	small cucumber, diced
2	pita breads
½	cup shredded lettuce
1	tablespoon nonfat yogurt
1	tablespoon bottled salsa

1. Season chicken breasts with chili powder, cumin, pepper, and salt. Set aside.

2. Heat a grill or broiler pan; grill or broil chicken breasts 3 minutes on each side (juices should run clear when pierced with a sharp knife.) Cut into strips; set aside.

3. Split pita breads open halfway. Divide shredded lettuce into each of 2 pitas.

4. Divide chicken strips and place in each pita. Top with tomato and cucumber.

5. Mix yogurt with salsa and pack in separate container. Tightly wrap each pita fajitta in aluminum foil. Chill fajitta and topping before packing in insulated bag.

Preparation time: 10 minutes
Cooking time: 6 minutes
Nutrients per serving:

Calories: 288	Sat. fat: less than 1 gm
Total fat: 2 gm	Cholesterol: 49 mg

Percentage of calories from fat: 6

Roast Beef and Coleslaw in Pita Pouch

The next time you make a roast beef for dinner save a few slices for the next day's lunch. The slaw both moistens and adds flavor to the meat. Kids love the pita pouch.

Makes 4 sandwiches

½ cup coleslaw
8 ounces lean cooked beef, cut into thin strips
4 6-inch whole wheat pita breads
1 ripe tomato, large enough for 8 slices
1 small cucumber, peeled and thinly sliced

1. Drain coleslaw.
2. Toss coleslaw with beef strips in a bowl.
3. Cut pita breads in halves.
4. Place one-fourth of filling in each bread half.
5. Top with tomato slices and cucumber and cover with remaining bread half. Wrap tightly in plastic wrap.

Preparation time: 10 minutes
Nutrients per serving:
  Calories: 219   Sat. fat: 2 gm
  Total fat: 9 gm   Cholesterol: 50 mg
      Percentage of calories from fat: 35

Raisin Bread and Cream Cheese

Little kids love cream cheese sandwiches. Although one third of fat is cut by using the "lite" cream cheese, use in moderation—it's still fattier than other sandwich fillings. A cup of soup is a nice accompaniment. Try an apple for dessert.

Makes 1 sandwich

2 tablespoons light cream cheese
4 walnut halves, chopped
2 tablespoons grated carrots
2 slices raisin bread

1. In a small bowl, mix cream cheese with nuts and carrots.

2. Spread one side of raisin bread with cream cheese mixture; top with another slice of raisin bread. Cut into squares or heart shapes. Wrap well in plastic wrap.

Preparation time: 5 minutes
Nutrients per serving:
  Calories: 244   Sat. fat: 6 gm
  Total fat: 11 gm   Cholesterol: 15 mg
            Percentage of calories from fat: 40

SOUPS

Whether eaten at home or packed in a Thermos on school days, soup is a wonderful way to offer youngsters a bowlful of nutrient-packed vegetables and is a great opportunity to introduce soluble fiber-rich beans. Best of all, soup is cheap and reusable, easy to freeze and heat up in the microwave. Also consider soup as an afternoon snack or a first course at dinnertime.

Turkey and Macaroni Soup

Kids love little meatballs. The balls here are made with low-fat turkey blended with egg whites. This is a great lunch-to-go suggestion with a few breadsticks and a chocolate cupcake for dessert.

Makes 6 servings

½   **pound ground white meat turkey**
1   **egg white**
3   **tablespoons seasoned breadcrumbs**
2   **tablespoons olive oil**
½   **cup chopped onions**
½   **cup shredded carrots**
½   **cup diced celery**
1   **tablespoon all-purpose flour**
4   **cups water**
3   **cups defatted beef broth**
1   **tablespoon Worcestershire sauce**
1   **bay leaf**
¼   **teaspoon dried basil**
1   **cup uncooked macaroni**
2   **tablespoons chopped parsley**

1. Preheat oven to 350° F. In a small bowl, mix together the turkey, egg white, and breadcrumbs. Shape into small balls.

2. Place turkey balls on a rack in a roasting pan and bake for about 20 minutes or until turkey starts to brown. Remove turkey and set aside.

3. In a large saucepan, heat oil, add vegetables, and cook, stirring often, until vegetables are tender, about 5 minutes. Stir in flour, mix well; add water and broth, Worcestershire sauce, bay leaf, basil, and cooked turkey balls. Mix well and simmer for about 10 to 15 minutes. Add the macaroni and continue cooking for 15 minutes, or until pasta is cooked al dente. Remove bay leaf. Top with parsley.

Preparation time: 10 minutes
Cooking time: 30 minutes for turkey balls
                    35 minutes for soup
Nutrients per serving:
    Calories: 162   Sat. fat: less than 1 gm
    Total fat: 5 gm   Cholesterol: 32 mg
              Percentage of calories from fat: 28

Hurry-Up Soup

*Pour 4 cups chicken broth into a 2-quart saucepan. Bring
to a boil. Remove from stove. Add to the soup pot: 1 cup
leftover cooked wagon wheel pasta or macaroni and 1 cup
frozen plain mixed vegetables. Reduce heat to low and simmer until vegetables are heated through. Spoon soup into
bowls or Thermos jars. Serve with whole-wheat breadsticks.*

Makes 4 servings

Preparation time: 3 minutes
Cooking time: 5 minutes
Nutrients per serving:
   Calories: 98   Sat. fat: None
   Total fat: 2 gm   Cholesterol: none
             Percentage of calories from fat: 16

Note: Canned broth is lower in salt content than chicken
bouillon from cubes, but Mom's homemade is best.

Quick Cannelini Soup

*Here's a fiber-rich bean soup that won raves from a group
of seven-year-old neighbors, who gulped up this soup on a
cold, snowy afternoon.*

Makes 4 servings

2   **tablespoons olive oil**
1   **cup onion, diced**
1   **clove garlic, minced**
½   **cup carrot, diced**
1   **16-ounce can cannelini beans, drained and**
        rinsed
2   **cups chicken broth, defatted**
2   **cups water**
2   **tablespoons chopped fresh parsley**
½   **teaspoon dried basil**
     Salt and pepper

1. In a 3-quart saucepan, heat oil, sauté onion, garlic, and carrot for about 3 minutes, stirring occasionally.
2. Add beans, broth, water, parsley, basil, and salt and pepper to taste.
3. Bring to a boil, stir, lower heat, cover, and simmer for 25 minutes. With slotted spoon, remove half of beans and puree in food processor with a little of the liquid. Return to soup pot; reheat before serving.

Preparation time: 15 minutes
Cooking time: 25 minutes
Nutrients per serving:
  Calories: 98   Sat. fat: none
  Total fat: 2 gm   Cholesterol: none
        Percentage of calories from fat: 16

Seafood Chowder

For kids who enjoy "creamy" soups, here's a low-fat version that uses skim milk, canned evaporated skim milk, and surimi (a shellfish look-alike that's made from low-fat white fleshed fish).

Makes 6 servings

1	tablespoon olive oil
1	cup chopped onion
1	cup chopped red pepper
½	cup chopped celery
2	tablespoons unbleached flour
2	cups chicken broth
2	cups skim milk
1	12-ounce can evaporated skim milk
8	ounces crab-flavored surimi, chunk style, cubed
2	cups frozen corn kernels
½	teaspoon black pepper

1. Heat oil in a large saucepan over medium heat. Add onions, peppers, and celery.

2. Cook over moderate heat for 4 to 6 minutes or until vegetables are soft.

3. Add flour to vegetable mixture and gradually add the chicken broth and bring to a boil.

4. Add skim milk, evaporated skim milk, surimi, corn, and pepper. Lower heat and cook, stirring occasionally, about 5 minutes or until chowder is heated through.

Preparation time: 10 minutes
Cooking time: 10 minutes
Nutrients per serving:
  Calories: 218   Sat. fat: less than 1 gm
  Total fat: 4 gm   Cholesterol: 16 mg
            Percentage of calories from fat: 16

Matthew's Favorite Soup

Eight-year-old Matthew Lipson enjoyed sampling many of the recipes being tested for the book. This vegetable soup was dubbed "awesome" by our pint-size critic. Matthew suggests that some kids might like the soup better without the chick-peas. The choice is yours.

Makes 6 servings

½   cup chopped onion
1   clove garlic
2   tablespoons olive oil
    Freshly ground pepper to taste
1   teaspoon dried basil
1   teaspoon dried oregano
½   cup diced carrot
½   cup diced celery
½   cup diced zucchini
2   cups chicken broth
4   cups water
1   16-ounce can tomatoes with liquid, broken into
     pieces
½   cup uncooked small-size macaroni
1   cup canned chick-peas, drained and rinsed
     (optional)

1. In a 3-quart saucepan, sauté onion and garlic in the olive oil until onion is soft; discard garlic.

2. Add pepper, basil, oregano, carrots, celery, zucchini, chicken broth, water, tomatoes, and uncooked macaroni, and chick-peas, if desired.

3. Bring to a boil, reduce heat, stir, cover, and simmer for 30 minutes, stirring occasionally.

Preparation time: 15 minutes
Cooking time: 40 minutes
Nutrients per serving:
    Calories: 162   Sat. fat: less than 1 gm
    Total fat: 6 gm   Cholesterol: none
          Percentage of calories from fat: 31

Manhattan Clam Chowder

This recipe is especially appealing to older kids. It's quick, tasty, and best of all, easy. You can eliminate or substitute diced vegetables—try diced turnips, green pepper, or zucchini.

Makes 4 servings

2	tablespoons olive oil
½	cup diced carrots
½	cup diced celery
½	cup diced potatoes
1	cup water
1	16-ounce can tomatoes, broken into pieces
⅛	teaspoon thyme
⅛	teaspoon pepper
2	tablespoons chopped fresh parsley
	8-ounce can minced clams, undrained

1. In the olive oil sauté carrots, celery, and potatoes for 3 minutes.

2. Add water, tomatoes (and liquid), plus thyme, pepper, and parsley.

3. Bring to a boil, lower heat, cover, and simmer for 15 minutes.

4. Add clams and continue to simmer 10 minutes longer, covered.

Preparation time: 10 minutes
Cooking time: 30 minutes
Nutrients per serving:

Calories: 136	Sat. fat: less than 1 gm
Total fat: 7 gm	Cholesterol: 18 mg
	Percentage of calories from fat: 48

SALADS

Salads can be a fun take-along for the lunch pail—especially for youngsters who like to pick at their food. To insure proper chilling, make the salad the night before and refrigerate overnight, then pack in insulated containers with the dressing on the side. Lettuce leaves can serve as scoops for eating salads instead of utensils.

Surimi and Tortellini Salad

Surimi is a shellfish "taste-alike," that is low in fat and is a good source of protein. It goes nicely with cheese tortellini (a cheese-filled pasta)—a combo that older children should enjoy. Carrots and red bell peppers add vitamins A and C, but the sky is the limit—add any combination your child prefers.

Makes 6 servings

1 10-ounce package cheese tortellini
1 cup plain low-fat yogurt
¼ cup reduced calorie mayonnaise
1 teaspoon vinegar
¼ teaspoon thyme
¼ teaspoon pepper
½ cup shredded carrots
1 cup red pepper strips
1 pound flaked crab-flavored surimi

1. Cook tortellini according to package directions.
2. In a small bowl combine yogurt, mayonnaise, vinegar, thyme. Stir until smooth.
3. In a large bowl, combine carrots, peppers, surimi, and dressing; mix well. Chill before serving.

Preparation time: 15 minutes, plus 1 hour chilling time.
Nutrients per serving:

Calories: 227	Sat. fat: 2 gm
Total fat: 6 gm	Cholesterol: 54 mg

Percentage of calories from fat: 24

Taco Salad

This is a fun salad—great for a weekend lunch. While corn tortillas have more fiber than white flour tortillas, the white flour ones work better to make the baked taco cup to fill with salad. Kids love the edible cup.

Makes 2 servings

2   **7- or 8-inch flour tortillas**
     Nonstick vegetable spray
2   **cups shredded lettuce**
2   **plum tomatoes, diced**
1   **cup total diced green or red pepper, onion, and
       cucumber**
½   **cup cooked kidney beans**
2   **tablespoons calorie reduced vinaigrette dressing**
2   **ounces part skim grated mozzarella cheese**
     Chopped onion for topping, optional

1. Preheat oven to 350° F. Brush tortillas with cool water to make them more manageable. Press each tortilla very gently into a small individual casserole (about 2-cup serving size) lightly sprayed with nonstick coating.

2. Bake for about 15 to 20 minutes or until light brown. Remove from casserole and allow to cool.

3. Meanwhile, in a bowl mix together shredded lettuce, tomatoes, mixed peppers, onions, cucumbers, and beans. Toss with dressing.

4. Place one tortilla cup on each plate and fill with salad. Allow salad to overflow onto plate. Top salad with grated mozzarella and chopped onion, if desired.

Preparation time: 25 minutes
Baking time: 20 minutes for taco shells
Nutrients per serving:
   Calories: 334   Sat. fat: 4 gm
   Total fat: 15 gm   Cholesterol: 16 mg
          Percentage of calories from fat: 33

Macaroni and Tuna Salad

When your youngster gets tired of plain old tuna sandwiches, try this. Pack in an insulated container. Add a bunch of grapes plus a couple of cookies to round out this lunch box menu.

Makes 1 serving

½ cup cooked macaroni
1 3-ounce can water-packed tuna, drained and
   flaked
2 teaspoons calorie reduced mayonnaise
¼ cup chopped celery
2 large leaves of romaine lettuce

1. Mix together macaroni with tuna, mayonnaise, and celery and place in chilled insulated container. Top with lettuce leaves which can be used for scooping.

Preparation time: 5 minutes
Nutrients per serving:
  Calories: 213   Sat. fat: less than 1 gm
  Total fat: 3 gm   Cholesterol: 35 mg
            Percentage of calories from fat: 15

Brown Bag Chef's Salad

Pack along a tangerine and a square of Banana Snack Cake for dessert.

Makes 1 serving

⅔   cup shredded romaine lettuce
2   tablespoons shredded carrots
2   green pepper rings
2   cherry tomatoes, cut in half
1   ounce low-fat Swiss cheese
2   ounces cooked turkey breast, cut in strips
1½   tablespoons bottled, reduced calorie Italian
         dressing

1. Place lettuce on bottom of container. Mix carrots, pepper, and tomato halves and place on top of lettuce.
2. Top with cheese and turkey, cover tightly. Chill.
3. Put dressing in separate, small container and pour over salad just before eating.

Preparation time: 10 minutes
Nutrients per serving:
  Calories: 217   Sat. fat: less than 1 gm
  Total fat: 8 gm   Cholesterol: 48 mg
          Percentage of calories from fat: 35

DINNER

Eating dinner together as a family whenever possible may be the single most important thing you can do to encourage healthy eating habits in your children. Remember that the habits kids learn at the dinner table last a lifetime.

Here are some simple ways to bring the family back to the dinner table.

- *Have fun while eating:* encourage pleasant talk, create a positive environment. Avoid criticism at the table. Children eat better when they come to the dinner table feeling relaxed.

- *Time meals appropriately:* make sure your child comes to the table rested. An overtired youngster can't appreciate the dinner hour, regardless of how tasty the meal. Avoid snacks or too much liquid right before mealtime. If you must serve dinner on the late side, offer a scheduled snack or a small portion of the prepared dinner meal at least an hour before you sit down to eat.

- *Limit distractions:* keep TV away from the table. Distracted children tend to forget about eating or may needlessly overeat.

- *Introduce new foods:* encourage your child to sample new foods in small amounts and only one at a time. Don't make a big deal about it. Sometimes serving new items along with more familiar ones encourages sampling.

- *Make dinner unintimidating:* serve finger foods and bite-sized pieces.

- *Make dinner appealing:* the better the food looks, the more likely it will be eaten. Set the table nicely—a small vase, a pretty place mat, even a colorful glass can all help make mealtime special.

- *Season lightly:* most children prefer mildly flavored foods, so use herbs, spices, salt, and pepper with discretion.

- *Never use food as a punishment—or reward:* teach children that food can be satisfying but don't encourage eating for emotional satisfaction when your youngster is sad. And never offer a food treat as a reward for being good.

- *Never frighten a child* by telling them that high-fat foods will give them a heart attack. Encourage choosing low-fat foods by saying "These foods help us grow up healthy—and big—and strong. Mommy and Daddy have learned to like these foods—so will you."

- *Get children involved* in shopping and cooking chores. The more hands-on experience, the greater the appreciation for food preparations.

"Oven-Fried" Fish

Fish is good for a heart-smart life-style, but not always popular with young children. This low-fat recipe should win favor in your household. This version offers a fried taste without the excess fat. The oat bran adds a boost of soluble fiber. Serve with mashed potatoes.

Makes 4 servings

1   pound fresh or frozen (thawed) haddock or
       similar firm, white fish fillets
2   tablespoons oat bran
¾   cup unbleached white flour
2   egg whites
½   cup skim milk
2   tablespoons margarine, melted
1   cup Italian-style bread crumbs
    Nonstick vegetable spray

1. Rinse and dry fish fillets. Preheat oven to 450° F.

2. Place oat bran and flour in a plastic bag; add fillets one at a time, and shake bag until fillets are well coated. Remove fillets and shake off excess flour.

3. With a fork, beat the egg whites and milk in a shallow pan.

4. Spread half the crumbs on a sheet of waxed paper. Dip the flour-coated fillets in the egg-milk mixture one at a time, until completely covered with liquid, allowing excess liquid to drip back into the pan.

5. Roll the fillets in bread crumbs until both sides are covered. Shake off excess. Add remainder of reserved crumbs to waxed paper as needed. (Recipe can be made in advance to this point. Cover and refrigerate fillets until ready to use.)

7. Place fillets on a baking sheet sprayed with nonstick vegetable spray, leaving space between each fish fillet. Drizzle the melted margarine over each fillet.

8. Bake fish fillets until coating begins to look lightly browned and crispy—about 5 minutes. Remove pan from oven, turn fillets over using a metal spatula, and continue to bake for an additional 5 minutes or until browned.

Preparation time: 10 minutes
Cooking time: 10 minutes
Nutrients per serving:
    Calories: 365   Sat. fat: 1 gm
      Total fat: 7 gm   Cholesterol: 83 mg
          Percentage of calories from fat: 17

Mashed Potatoes

Much lower in fat and calories than most mashed potato recipes, this recipe is made, with yogurt, which gives it a rich, creamy texture. We found this dish tasted even better a day after; somehow the "yogurt-y" taste disappears.

Makes 8 servings

1	tablespoon olive oil
1	tablespoon minced garlic
4	cups water
4	medium size russet potatoes, peeled and cut into quarters (about 2 to 2¼ pounds)
1	cup plain low-fat yogurt
¼	cup skim milk
1	teaspoon salt, or to taste
¼	teaspoon pepper, or to taste

1. Heat oil over medium-low heat in a heavy saucepan. Add garlic and sauté 1 minute, stirring constantly, until fragrant, but not browned. Add water and potatoes.

2. Cover and bring to a boil over high heat. Reduce heat to medium low and simmer 15 to 20 minutes, or until potatoes are tender.

3. Drain well through a large, fine-meshed sieve. Return potatoes to pan and mash away from heat. Add yogurt and milk and stir until creamy. Add salt and pepper to taste. Reheat if needed.

Preparation time: 15 minutes
Cooking time: 20 minutes
Nutrients per serving:
  Calories: 126   Sat. fat: less than 1 gm
  Total fat: 2 gm   Cholesterol: 2 mg
            Percentage of calories from fat: 17

Turkey Chili in a Cup

Beans are important for heart-healthy eating. If your child resists, try them disguised in this delicious chili. For added kid appeal serve in a baked tortilla shell with carrot sticks and zucchini spears. For dessert, try a slice of ginger cake with pear apple sauce.

Makes 4 servings

4	7- or 8-inch flour tortillas
	Nonstick vegetable spray
1	pound ground turkey
½	cup chopped onion
1½	cups no-salt-added tomato sauce
2	teaspoons chili powder, or to taste
½	teaspoon cumin
2	cups cooked kidney beans (if using canned, rinse and drain)
1	4-ounce can chopped green chili peppers

1. Preheat oven to 350° F. Brush tortillas with cold water to make them more manageable.

2. Press each tortilla very gently into a small individual ovenproof casserole (about 2 cups serving size) lightly sprayed with nonstick vegetable spray and bake for 15 to 20 minutes.

3. In the meantime, brown the turkey and onion in a fry pan sprayed with nonstick vegetable spray. Drain off excess fat. Stir in tomato sauce, chili powder, and cumin; bring to a boil. Reduce heat.

4. Add beans and chopped peppers. Cook 10 to 15 minutes, uncovered, stirring occasionally.

5. Fill cups with chili.

Preparation time: 15 minutes
Cooking time: 15 minutes (plus 20 minutes to bake tortillas)
Nutrients per serving:
  Calories: 478   Sat. fat: 5 gm
  Total fat: 13 gm   Cholesterol: 76 mg
        Percentage of calories from fat: 24

Beef and Broccoli Stir-fry

This colorful stir-fry is perfect for heart-healthy eating. It provides small portions of lean meat combined with broccoli for vitamins, minerals, and fiber. Serve over brown rice to round out the meal.

Makes 6 servings

1	pound boneless flank steak or top round steak
⅓	cup water
1	tablespoon plus 1 teaspoon cornstarch
4	tablespoons sodium-reduced soy sauce
½	cup dry sherry or chicken broth
1½	teaspoons ground ginger
1	teaspoon garlic powder
2	tablespoons canola or peanut oil
2	10-ounce packages frozen broccoli florets, partially thawed
1	cup canned water chestnuts, drained and sliced

1. Trim all visible fat from meat, then freeze for about 1 hour. When firm, slice meat across the grain into strips 1 inch long by ⅛ inch thick.

2. In a small bowl, mix water with cornstarch until smooth. Mix in soy sauce, sherry or broth, ginger, and garlic powder.

3. In a wok, heavy skillet, or electric skillet, heat 1 tablespoon oil until very hot. Add half the meat, stirring constantly, until it is lightly browned. Remove from pan and cook second batch without adding more oil.

4. Remove second batch of meat from pan, add 1 tablespoon oil, and add broccoli. Cook briefly, stirring constantly, then return meat to pan. Add water chestnuts and cornstarch mixture.

5. Bring to a boil while stirring. Continue cooking and stirring until sauce is thickened and clear. Serve with brown rice.

Preparation time: 15 minutes plus 1 hour to freeze meat
Cooking time: 10 minutes
Nutrients per serving:
   Calories: 271   Sat. fat: 5 gm
   Total fat: 15 gm   Cholesterol: 39 mg
          Percentage of calories from fat: 47

Macaroni and Cheese

Here's a comfort food with half the fat of the traditional recipe. For the defatted version, we use skim milk and reduced-calorie cheese. Try it as a side dish or as a main dish for a light supper. Add a tossed salad and a bowl of vegetable soup.

Makes 6 servings

2   tablespoons margarine
2   tablespoons flour
    Salt and white pepper to taste
2½ cups skim milk
1   teaspoon dry mustard
2   cups (8 ounces) shredded reduced-calorie
      cheddar cheese
4   cups cooked elbow macaroni
    Nonstick vegetable spray
1   tablespoon seasoned bread crumbs

1. Preheat oven to 375° F. In a medium saucepan, melt margarine; stir in flour and salt and pepper as desired. Gradually stir in milk and mustard and cook until mixture coats back of a spoon.
2. Remove from heat and stir in 1½ cups cheese and the macaroni.
3. Spray a 1½ quart baking dish with nonstick spray; pour in cheese and macaroni mixture.
4. Top with remaining ½ cup cheese and bread crumbs. Bake for 20 minutes.

Preparation time: 20 minutes
Baking time: 20 minutes
Nutrients per serving:
  Calories: 310   Sat. fat: 5 gm
  Total fat: 11 gm   Cholesterol: 29 mg
            Percentage of calories from fat: 34

Orange Chicken Cutlets

White meat chicken cutlets can often be too dry to be very appealing. The orange sauce puts back some of the zing.

Makes 4 servings

1   **pound skinless chicken cutlets**
2   **tablespoons flour**
     Salt and pepper to taste
1   **tablespoon margarine**
1   **tablespoon honey**
1   **teaspoon reduced sodium soy sauce**
½   **cup orange juice**
2   **tablespoons chopped onion, optional**
1   **teaspoon cornstarch**
1   **tablespoon water**
2   **teaspoons sliced almonds, optional**

1. Rinse and pat dry cutlets. Dust with flour mixed with salt and pepper.

2. Heat margarine in skillet and brown cutlets for about 3 minutes on each side, or until cutlets are cooked through and golden; set aside.

3. In a small dish, mix honey, soy sauce, orange juice, and onion. Heat in a small pan; add cornstarch blended with water and cook, stirring constantly until mixture thickens. Pour over cutlets; garnish with almonds.

Preparation time: 10 minutes
Cooking time: 15 minutes
Nutrients per serving:

Calories: 212	Sat. fat: less than 1 gm
Total fat: 4 gm	Cholesterol: 66 mg

Percentage of calories from fat: 19

Noodle Pudding

Here's a rich, tasty noodle pudding made with eggless egg noodles and low-fat dairy products. The noodle product is called No Yolks and is available in major supermarkets. These noodles are cholesterol free; regular egg noodles contain more than 50 milligrams of cholesterol per serving. Use as a side dish for roasted chicken or as is for a light supper.

Makes 6 servings

⅓   of 12-ounce package (or 4 ounces) cholesterol-free egg noodles
½   cup light ricotta cheese
½   cup skim milk
4   egg whites, slightly beaten
3   tablespoons honey
¼   teaspoon ground cinnamon, divided in half
1   medium pear, chopped
¼   cup finely chopped dried apricots
    Nonstick vegetable spray
1   tablespoon sugar

1. Preheat oven to 350° F. Cook noodles according to package directions. Meanwhile, combine ricotta, milk, egg whites, honey, and ⅛ teaspoon cinnamon; stir until well blended. Stir in pear and apricots.

2. Drain noodles. Combine with ricotta mixture. Pour into 2-quart casserole coated with nonstick vegetable spray.

3. Combine sugar and remaining ⅛ teaspoon cinnamon. Sprinkle evenly over top of noodles. Bake for 25 to 30 minutes or until set.

4. Allow to stand 10 minutes before serving. May be served warm or chilled.

Preparation time: 20 minutes
Baking time: 30 minutes
Nutrients per serving:
   Calories: 181   Sat. fat: 1 gm
   Total fat: 2 gm   Cholesterol: 7 mg
          Percentage of calories from fat: 9

Tamale Pie

Here's a recipe from a cooking class given by the American Heart Association. I tried it for dinner one night and got raves from two of my three children. Laurie refused to eat it when she realized the dish included raisins.

Now that she's a grown-up, she makes it for her family— without the raisins. It works fine. Serve with a green salad. For dessert, offer peaches canned in light syrup and a few oatmeal cookies.

Makes 8 servings

2½	cups beef broth
1	cup yellow cornmeal
2	tablespoons corn or canola oil
1	medium onion, chopped
3	cloves garlic, minced
1	pound ground turkey
1½	cups chopped tomatoes, fresh or canned
4	tablespoons tomato paste
1	teaspoon dried oregano
½	teaspoon ground cumin
1	tablespoon chili powder
1½ to 2	cups corn, drained
⅓	cup sliced, stuffed green olives
⅓	cup raisins, plumped in hot water and drained
1	4-ounce can green chilies, drained and chopped
2	tablespoons grated Parmesan cheese

1. Preheat oven to 350° F. In a large saucepan, combine ½ cup broth with the cornmeal. In a separate pan, bring the remainder of the broth to a boil. Stir into the cornmeal. Cover, cook over medium heat, stirring occasionally, until the mixture thickens, about 10 minutes. Set aside to cool.

2. In a skillet, heat the oil and lightly brown the onion and garlic. Add the turkey in small chunks; cook until meat turns white. Drain off any grease.

3. Add tomatoes, tomato paste, oregano, cumin, and chili powder. Simmer 5 minutes. If sauce is too thin, add additional tomato paste. Add corn, olives, raisins, and chilies. Stir gently.

4. Line the bottom and sides of a 2½-quart casserole with the reserved cornmeal mush. Spoon in the filling and sprinkle with Parmesan cheese. Bake for 30 minutes.

Preparation time: 30 minutes
Cooking time: 50 minutes
Nutrients per serving:
  Calories: 277   Sat. fat: 3 gm
  Total fat: 11 gm   Cholesterol: 39 mg
             Percentage of calories from fat: 36

Sweet and Sour Turkey Meatballs

Kids love meatballs, but traditional recipes are loaded with fat. This sweet and sour recipe, made with turkey, is guaranteed to please young palates. Serve over brown rice.

Makes 4 servings

1	pound ground turkey
3	tablespoons bread crumbs
1	egg white, slightly beaten
2	tablespoons chopped onion
¼	teaspoon garlic powder
⅛	teaspoon pepper
	Nonstick vegetable spray
1	16-ounce can whole-berry cranberry sauce
1	12-ounce bottle chili sauce

1. Preheat oven to 350° F.

2. Combine turkey, bread crumbs, and egg white in a medium-size bowl. Mix in chopped onion, garlic powder, and pepper. Roll into balls.

3. Place meatballs on a rack coated with nonstick vegetable spray. Place rack on a shallow roasting pan and bake for 20 minutes. Set aside.

4. In the meantime, combine cranberry and chili sauces in a saucepan and cook over low heat for about 10 minutes, allowing flavors to blend.

5. Add cooked meatballs and continue to simmer, covered, for an additional 15 minutes. Serve over brown rice.

Preparation time: 20 minutes
Cooking time: 30 minutes (including baking time)
Nutrients per serving:
  Calories: 431   Sat. fat: 4 gm
  Total fat: 11 gm   Cholesterol: 72 mg
          Percentage of calories from fat: 22

Pasta Primavera with Chicken

Here's a good way to offer dinner in a wok, the Chinese cooking pot. No wok? No problem. Simply use a large skillet. And if your youngster doesn't go for some of the vegetables suggested here, feel free to substitute. The dish will be just as tasty and nutritious.

Makes 6 servings

1	pound boneless, skinless chicken breasts
2	tablespoons peanut or canola oil
4	green onions, cut in julienne strips (about ½ cup)
1	clove garlic, minced or pressed
2	cups julienned zucchini
2	carrots, peeled, and julienned (about 1 cup)
½	cup chicken broth
½	cup orange juice
¼	cup chopped fresh parsley
½	teaspoon dried oregano
⅛	teaspoon ground pepper
½	pound spaghetti, cooked and drained
⅓	cup freshly grated Parmesan cheese

1. Rinse chicken and pat dry; slice into thin strips.

2. In large skillet, over medium-high heat, heat 1 tablespoon oil. Stir-fry chicken, add green onions and garlic; cook 1 minute, stirring frequently.

3. Remove chicken and green onions, set aside.

4. Heat remaining oil in skillet, add zucchini and carrots and cook 2 minutes, stirring frequently. Return chicken and green onions to skillet.

5. Stir in broth, juice, parsley, oregano, and pepper, simmer 1 to 2 minutes or until vegetables are tender-crisp.

6. Place spaghetti on large platter, top with chicken mixture. Sprinkle with cheese. Toss and serve.

Preparation time: 25 minutes
Cooking time: 10 minutes
Nutrients per serving:
    Calories: 318   Sat. fat: 2 gm
    Total fat: 8 gm   Cholesterol: 48 mg
        Percentage of calories from fat: 22

Vegetable Pork Stew

Over the years, hogs have gone on a diet and pork is getting leaner. Here's a stew that's quick to prepare using the leanest cut, pork tenderloin. Youngsters may enjoy helping you add the pepper, corn, onions, and parsley to the pot. Serve with mini corn muffins.

Makes 4 servings

1	tablespoon, plus 1 teaspoon canola oil
1	pound fat-trimmed boneless pork tenderloin, cut into cubes
1	large onion, coarsely sliced
1	clove garlic, chopped fine
1	16-ounce can tomatoes
1	sweet red bell pepper, coarsely chopped
1	cup frozen corn kernels
2	tablespoons chopped fresh parsley
½	teaspoon dried cumin
½	teaspoon dried oregano
¼	teaspoon dried thyme
	Freshly ground pepper to taste

1. In a heavy saucepan or nonstick skillet, heat oil over medium-high heat; add pork a few cubes at a time, cooking until meat is lightly browned.

2. Add onion and garlic. Cook, stirring, about 2 minutes.

3. Add tomatoes, pepper, corn, parsley, cumin, oregano, thyme, and ground pepper to taste. Bring to a boil; reduce heat and simmer covered for 20 minutes.

Preparation time: 20 minutes
Cooking time: 30 minutes
Nutrients per serving:
   Calories: 248   Sat. fat: 1 gm
   Total fat: 8 gm   Cholesterol: 74 mg
          Percentage of calories from fat: 29

Mini Cornbread Muffins

You will need a mini-muffin tin to make this easy "go with."
Kids love midget-sized foods!

Makes 24 mini-muffins

1   cup yellow corn meal
1   cup sifted unbleached flour
¼   cup sugar
1   tablespoon baking powder
1   teaspoon salt
¼   cup tub margarine
1   egg, beaten
1   cup skim milk

1. Preheat oven to 350° F. Combine corn meal, flour, sugar, baking powder, and salt in a bowl. Using two knives, add in margarine, mixing until crumbly.

2. Mix egg and milk together and add to dry ingredients with a few strokes. Fill slightly oiled mini-muffin tins two-thirds full.

3. Bake for about 15 minutes or until tester comes out clean.

Preparation time: 10 minutes
Cooking time: 15 minutes
Nutrients per muffin:
   Calories: 70   Sat. fat: less than 1 gm
   Total fat: 2 gm   Cholesterol: 9 mg
        Percentage of calories from fat: 27

Heart-Smart Hamburgers

Juicy, delicious, fiber rich—all for under 33 percent fat calories per serving. Bulgar wheat adds fiber plus vitamins and minerals to the hamburgers; but don't worry, no one will recognize the mystery ingredient.

Makes 6 servings

1	egg white, slightly beaten
⅓	cup bulgur wheat
¼	cup ketchup
1	teaspoon dried Italian seasoning, crushed
½	teaspoon dillweed
⅛	teaspoon pepper
	Salt to taste
1	pound lean ground round
6	whole wheat hamburger buns, split and toasted
	Romaine lettuce leaves
6	tomato slices
	Alfalfa sprouts, optional

1. In a medium-size mixing bowl, combine egg white, bulgur, ketchup, Italian seasoning, dillweed, pepper, and salt.

2. Add beef and mix well.

3. Shape mixture into six ½-inch thick patties.

4. Place patties on unheated rack of a broiler pan or on a preheated grill. Broil 3 inches from heat for about 12 minutes, turning once.

5. Serve on buns with lettuce, tomato, and sprouts if desired.

Preparation time: 5 minutes
Cooking time: 10 to 12 minutes
Nutrients per serving:
    Calories: 285   Sat. fat: 4 gm
    Total fat: 11 gm   Cholesterol: 48 mg
          Percentage of calories from fat: 33

Turkey Parmesan

This recipe works best when the cutlets are made in advance and frozen. All you need to do is remove cutlets from freezer, top with sauce and cheese, and bake.

Makes 4 servings

Prepare Ahead

1	egg white
1	tablespoon water
½	cup seasoned bread crumbs
1	pound turkey breast cutlets or slices, ⅛-inch to ⅜-inch thick.

Before Serving

4	ounces part skim mozzarella cheese
¾	cup tomato sauce

1. In shallow bowl, beat egg white and water together. Set aside.

2. Spread bread crumbs over shallow plate.

3. Dip turkey cutlets into egg mixture, let excess drip off, and then dip cutlets into crumb mixture, making sure both sides are well coated.

4. Arrange cutlets on a cookie sheet. Freeze 30 to 45 minutes. Transfer frozen turkey slices to self-closing freezer bag and return to freezer until ready to bake.

5. When ready to serve, preheat oven to 350° F. Place cutlets in a baking pan, top each cutlet with 1 ounce part skim mozzarella cheese and 3 tablespoons of tomato sauce. Bake until cheese is hot and bubbly and cutlet is cooked through, about 15 minutes.

Preparation time: 20 minutes (plus 40 minutes for freezing)
Cooking time: 15 minutes
Nutrients per serving:

Calories: 282	Sat. fat: 4 gm
Total fat: 8 gm	Cholesterol: 87 mg

Percentage of calories from fat: 26

Glazed Sweet Potatoes

Once you slice the potatoes, even a preschooler will be able to help assemble this easy-to-make side dish. Kids will love the bright color. Serve with turkey or chicken.

Makes 4 servings

1   **pound sweet potatoes, peeled and cut into**
       ½-inch thick slices
       Nonstick vegetable spray
1   **tablespoon cornstarch**
1   **tablespoon brown sugar**
¾   **cup orange juice**
2   **tablespoons lemon juice**

1. Preheat oven to 425° F. Place sliced potatoes in a 1-quart, flat casserole coated with cooking spray.

2. Combine cornstarch and brown sugar in a small bowl. Add the orange and lemon juices, stirring well.

3. Pour over potatoes and bake for about 40 minutes or until potatoes are just tender and glaze is thickened, stirring sauce once or twice.

Preparation time: 10 minutes
Cooking time: 45 minutes
Nutrients per serving:
   Calories: 130   Sat. fat: none
   Total fat: less than   Cholesterol: none
     1 gm
         Percentage of calories from fat: 4

DESSERTS

Dessert time is special for children. But all too often desserts are laden with fat and empty sugar calories. Of course, luscious, ripe fruit of the season makes a healthful alternative, but if your youngster thinks of dessert as cakes, puddings, ice cream, and cookies, take heart. You'll find delicious low-fat versions of traditional recipes in this section, including blueberry cobbler, chocolate pudding, gingerbread, and and even a banana split! We also offer two versions of a crunchy meringue cookie, one studded with walnuts, and the other totally fat free.

In between these special treats, do try to serve more fruit. While fresh is always best, canned and frozen fruits are fine, too, as long as they are packed in unsweetened natural juices. So keep a bowl of fresh fruit out at all times, and after dinner, bring out the peaches and pears, slice up an apple, cube a ripe melon, and put out the plums.

Chocolate Pudding

A family favorite for young and old. Here's a delicious low-fat version.

Makes 4 servings

3 tablespoons unsweetened cocoa powder
¼ cup sugar
3 tablespoons cornstarch
2 cups 1 percent milk
1 teaspoon vanilla

1. Combine cocoa, sugar, and cornstarch in medium saucepan. Gradually stir in milk.

2. Cook over medium heat, stirring constantly, until mixture boils; boil and stir 1 minute.

3. Remove from heat; stir in vanilla. Pour into serving bowls. Press plastic wrap onto surfaces. Cool. Chill.

Preparation time: 5 minutes
Cooking time: 5 minutes (plus 1 hour chilling time)
Nutrients per serving:

Calories: 136	Sat. fat: 1 gm
Total fat: 2 gm	Cholesterol: 5 mg

Percentage of calories from fat: 13

Blueberry Cobbler

This dessert is best when blueberries are in season, but frozen berries are also good. Like all berries, blueberries are a good source of dietary fiber. Try serving with a dollop of vanilla yogurt—no one will miss the ice cream.

Makes 8 servings

⅓   **cup sugar**
1   **tablespoon cornstarch**
¾   **cup orange juice**
2½ **cups fresh blueberries**
1   **cup all-purpose flour**
1½ **teaspoons baking powder**
⅓   **cup skim milk**
3   **tablespoons corn oil**
1   **teaspoon sugar**

1. Preheat oven to 325° F. In a small saucepan, stir together sugar and cornstarch, then add the orange juice. Cook and stir until thickened and bubbly. Add blueberries; cook until berries are hot. Keep warm.

2. Stir together flour and baking powder. Add milk and oil; stir until mixture forms a ball. On a lightly floured surface, pat into an 8-inch circle, then cut into eight wedges.

3. Spoon hot berry mixture into a 9-inch pie plate and immediately top with wedges of dough. Sprinkle with 1 teaspoon sugar. Bake for 25 or 30 minutes or until wedges are brown. Serve warm.

Preparation time: 15 minutes
Cooking time: 30 minutes
Nutrients per serving:
  Calories: 179   Sat. fat: less than 1 gm
  Total fat: 6 gm   Cholesterol: less than 1 mg
          Percentage of calories from fat: 27

Banana Split

The chocolate sauce is made with cocoa and buttermilk (naturally low in fat) instead of chocolate and cream. Ice milk instead of ice cream cuts the fat even more. But when it comes to flavor, nothing is lost.

Makes 4 servings

⅓   **cup unsweetened cocoa powder**
¼   **cup packed light brown sugar**
½   **cup buttermilk**
2   **medium-size bananas, each split lengthwise, then cut in half crosswise**
1   **pint vanilla ice milk**
1   **cup light canned peaches, drained**
4   **vanilla wafer cookies**

1. Mix cocoa and brown sugar in a small saucepan. Add buttermilk and stir over medium-low heat 3 to 4 minutes until sugar melts and mixture is smooth. Let cool.

2. Place 2 pieces of banana in each of 4 dessert dishes. Add 2 scoops ice milk. Spoon on 1 tablespoon chocolate sauce and 3 tablespoons peaches and top with cookies.

Preparation time: 10 minutes
Cooking time: 4 minutes
Nutrients per serving:

   Calories: 268   Sat. fat: 3 gm
   Total fat: 5 gm   Cholesterol: 12 mg
         Percentage of calories from fat: 16

Fresh Pear Crisp

Here's a good recipe when pears are in season. Kids like the crunchy texture of the topping.

Makes 9 servings

½	**cup unsifted flour**
½	**cup quick oats**
½	**cup firmly packed brown sugar**
½	**teaspoon ground cinnamon**
¼	**cup unsalted margarine**
2	**pounds pears, peeled, cored, and thinly sliced (about 4½ cups)**
1	**tablespoon lemon juice**
2	**teaspoons sugar**
1	**teaspoon grated lemon rind**
¼	**teaspoon ground ginger**

1. Preheat oven to 350° F. Stir together flour, oats, brown sugar, cinnamon. With a pastry blender, cut in margarine until coarse crumbs form.

2. In an 8-by–12-inch baking dish, toss pears and lemon juice. Sprinkle on sugar, lemon rind, and ginger; toss to coat.

3. Spoon crumb mixture over pears. Bake for 45 minutes or until golden.

Preparation time: 15 minutes
Baking time: 45 minutes
Nutrients per serving:
   Calories: 192   Sat. fat: 1 gm
   Total fat: 6 gm   Cholesterol: none
            Percentage of calories from fat: 26

Fruit Kabobs with Creamy Dip

Kids love finger food. Here's a fun way to encourage eating a variety of fruits.

Makes 8 servings

Half of an 8-ounce can unsweetened pineapple chunks
1   medium apple, unpeeled and cored
1   tangerine, divided into sections (about 8)
1   small banana, cut into 8 ½-inch slices
1   kiwi, cut into 8 slices
4   fresh strawberries, each cut in half lengthwise

1. Drain pineapple, reserving juice. Set aside 8 pineapple chunks, plus ¼ cup juice, reserving remaining pineapple and juice for another dessert.

2. Cut apple into 8 1-inch chunks. Thread fruit onto 8 6-inch-long plastic drinking straws. Brush with reserved ¼ cup pineapple juice. Serve with creamy dip.

Preparation time: 10 minutes
Nutrients per serving:
   Calories: 38   Sat. fat: none
   Total fat: Cholesterol: none
     less than 1 g
            Percentage of calories from fat: 3

Creamy Dip

*Makes ½ cup or about
1 tablespoon per kabob*

¼   **cup light cream cheese**
¼   **cup banana low-fat yogurt**
2   **tablespoons marshmallow cream**

1. Combine all ingredients in a small mixing bowl. Beat at low speed with an electric mixer until well blended. Cover and chill about 2 hours.

Preparation time: 10 minutes, plus 2 hours chilling time.
Nutrients per serving for 1 tablespoon serving:
  Calories: 32   Sat. fat: 1 gm
  Total fat: 2 gm   Cholesterol: 7 mg
            Percentage of calories from fat: 52

"Don't Tell 'em What's in 'em" Brownies

Your family will never know that these chocolaty confections are made with grated zucchini and whole wheat flour. But you'll know they are getting an extra vitamin boost. Still, eat in moderation. While these cholesterol-free goodies are much lower in fat then regular brownies, which average 54 percent calories from fat, they still derive 36 percent of their calories from fat.

Makes 16 servings

4   **egg whites**
1   **medium size zucchini (about 1 cup grated)**
1   **cup whole wheat flour**
1   **cup sugar**
⅓   **cup cocoa powder**
½   **teaspoon baking powder**
⅓   **cup vegetable oil**
1   **teaspoon vanilla extract**
¼   **cup walnuts or other nuts (optional)**

1. Preheat oven to 350° F. In food processor or blender, whip egg whites. Then add grated zucchini until finely chopped.

2. Sift dry ingredients together in a mixing bowl. Stir in oil, vanilla, nuts, if using, and zucchini–egg white mixture just until blended. Don't overmix. Pour into lightly oiled 8-inch square baking pan and bake for 30 to 35 minutes. Cool and cut into 16 squares.

Preparation time: 15 minutes
Cooking time: 35 minutes
Nutrients per brownie:

Calories: 124	Sat. fat: less than 1 gm
Total fat: 5 gm	Cholesterol: none

Percentage of calories from fat: 36

Banana Snack Cake

A tasty way to use up ripe bananas. Snack cakes pack well, so add to your youngster's lunch box.

Makes 12 servings

Nonstick vegetable spray
1½ cup flour
½   cup sugar
1   teaspoon baking powder
½   teaspoon baking soda
1   teaspoon cinnamon
¼   teaspoon salt
1   cup bananas, ripe, mashed (1 to 2 bananas)
¼   cup vanilla low-fat yogurt
¼   cup canola oil
1   egg slightly beaten
1   teaspoon vanilla

1. Preheat oven to 350° F. Spray a 9-by-9-inch pan with nonstick vegetable spray.

2. Mix dry ingredients thoroughly.

3. Mix remaining ingredients; add to dry ingredients. Stir until dry ingredients are barely moistened.

4. Pour into pan. Bake 20 minutes or until toothpick inserted in center comes out clean.

Preparation time: 10 minutes
Cooking time: 20 minutes
Nutrients per serving:
  Calories: 159   Sat. fat: less than 1 gm
  Total fat: 5 gm   Cholesterol: 18 mg
        Percentage of calories from fat: 30

Gingerbread with Pear Applesauce

Here's a family favorite developed by experts at project LEAN—a nationwide network of health agencies banded together to urge Low-fat Eating for Americans Now. While this fabulous dessert is quite low in fat, it is not low in calories, so don't allow your youngster to go overboard if you're concerned about his or her weight.

Makes 12 servings

	Nonstick vegetable spray
2¾	cups unsifted all-purpose flour
1	cup sugar
1	teaspoon baking soda
¼	teaspoon salt
1	teaspoon ground cinnamon
¼	teaspoon ground nutmeg
¼	teaspoon ground cloves
¼	teaspoon ground allspice
1	cup blackstrap molasses
1	cup low-fat buttermilk
⅓	cup canola oil
1	tablespoon freshly grated gingerroot
1	cup dried currants which have been soaked in 2 tablespoons hot water

1. Adjust oven rack to lower third of oven. Preheat oven to 325° F. Spray a 9-by-9-by-2-inch square pan with non-stick vegetable spray; line bottom with waxed paper.

2. Stir flour, sugar, baking soda, salt, and spices into large mixing bowl. Beat together molasses, buttermilk, oil, and ginger. Add to flour mixture; mix until blended. Stir in currants.

3. Pour into prepared pan. Bake for 1 hour and 10 minutes or until a tester inserted in center comes out clean. Run flexible spatula around edge of cake. Invert cake onto wire rack. Discard waxed paper liner. Cool completely.

4. Cut into squares or wedges. Serve Pear Applesauce alongside cake.

Pear Applesauce

1   **pound each Comice pears and McIntosh apples, peeled and cored**
1   **tablespoon sugar**
2   **tablespoons water**

1. Cut pears and apples into slices.

2. In a large saucepan, combine pears, apples, sugar, and water.

3. Cook over medium heat, stirring occasionally, until liquid is absorbed.

Preparation time: 30 minutes
Cooking time: 90 minutes, plus 10 minutes for applesauce.
Nutrients per serving for gingerbread and pear applesauce:

Calories: 366	Sat. fat: less than 1 gm
Total fat: 6 gm	Cholesterol: less than 1 mg

Percentage of calories from fat: 16

Meringue Cookies

Kids love to watch the egg white froth and triple in volume as you prepare these cookies. For youngsters who love chocolate, subsitute chocolate chips for the nuts. For a version that's 100 percent fat free, eliminate the nuts and fold in a tablespoon of cocoa powder when adding the orange juice.

Makes 30 cookies

2   egg whites
6   tablespoons sugar
1   teaspoon white vinegar
1   teaspoon orange juice
½   cup coarsely chopped walnuts

1. Preheat oven to 225° F. In a large mixing bowl, combine the egg whites and sugar and warm gently over hot water bath to dissolve the sugar into the egg whites. When liquid becomes clear, remove from water bath.
2. Using an electric mixer, whip egg whites and sugar mixture at high speed until the mixture is of a stiff, gooey, consistency.
3. Fold in vinegar, juice, and nuts. Drop by rounded teaspoonfuls onto a greased cookie sheet and bake for 1½ hours or until cookies are dry. Cool on tray.

Preparation time: 10 minutes
Cooking time: 1½ hours
Nutrients per cookie:
  Calories: 26   Sat. fat: less than 1 gm
  Total fat: 1 gm   Cholesterol: none
              Percentage of calories from fat: 35

Chips 'n' Oats Freezer Cookies

This delicious frozen "slice and bake" cookie dough is much healthier than the commercial recipe.

Makes about 64 cookies

2	cups unbleached flour
1	teaspoon baking powder
½	teaspoon salt
1	scant teaspoon allspice
½	cup canola oil
½	cup low-fat plain yogurt
1	cup sugar
2	eggs, slightly beaten
1	teaspoon vanilla
3	cups rolled oats
½	cup raisins
¼	cup semi-sweet chocolate chips

1. In a bowl, mix flour, baking powder, salt, and allspice. In another bowl, mix oil and yogurt. Add eggs and vanilla. Mix well. Stir in dry ingredients. Add oats, raisins, and chocolate chips. Blend well.

2. Divide dough into 5 parts; shape each into a log, 6 inches long by 1½ inches in diameter. Wrap in waxed paper to freeze.

3. When ready to bake, preheat oven to 350° F. Lightly grease baking sheet. Remove roll from freezer and cut into thin slices. Place on baking sheet; bake for about 15 minutes or until lightly browned.

Preparation time: 20 minutes
Cooking time: 15 minutes
Nutrients per cookie:

Calories: 66	Sat. fat: less than 1 gm
Total fat: 2 gm	Cholesterol: 7 mg

Percentage of calories from fat: 32

"Naturally Sweet" Cookies

These cookies get their natural sweetness and fiber from raisins, dates, banana, and oatmeal. A truly delicious sugarless cookie, they make a fine lunch box treat.

Makes 40 cookies

½   cup raisins
½   cup packed chopped dates
1   medium-size ripe banana, sliced
⅓   cup creamy peanut butter
¼   cup water
1   egg
1   teaspoon vanilla
1   cup oatmeal
½   cup flour
1   teaspoon baking soda

1. Preheat oven to 350° F.
2. In mixing bowl, combine raisins, dates, banana, peanut butter, water, egg, and vanilla. Beat until blended.
3. Add oatmeal, flour, and baking soda. Mix to blend thoroughly. Drop by teaspoonfuls onto nonstick baking sheets or baking sheets coated with nonstick vegetable spray; flatten slightly.
4. Bake about 10 minutes until browned on underside. Cool on racks. Store in airtight container.

Preparation time: 15 minutes
Baking time: 10 minutes
Nutrients per cookie:
   Calories: 42   Sat. fat: less than 1 gm
   Total fat: 1 gm   Cholesterol: 5 mg
          Percentage of calories from fat: 28

SNACKS

Snacks are an important part of a child's overall diet—on average, kids get 25 to 30 percent of their daily calories from snacks. This is largely because most youngsters have a relatively small eating capacity at any given time and can't pack in all the calories and nutrients they need at breakfast, lunch, and dinner.

Remember, though, that snack time is not simply any old time—it should be a scheduled time of day between but not too close to meals. Let your youngster help choose the time and foods he will eat.

For most kids, an after-school snack is essential—a good time to relax and refuel. Depending on your youngster's age and appetite, it can be anything from a glass of low-fat milk and a cookie or a bowl of vegetable soup and breadstick to a pita pizza. Many need a mid-morning snack as well, especially if breakfast is skimpy or eaten very early, or a snack before going to bed. Regardless of the time of day eaten, snacks should be built around low-fat nutrient-packed foods—never junk foods.

Why not begin by trying the delicious recipes in this section, which are sure to please both you and your youngster?

Quick Snacks

Even when there's no time—take time for snacking. Here are a few suggestions that will take less than 10 minutes to prepare:

- mash one half banana with 1 tablespoon peanut butter and spread on raisin cinnamon bagel

- spread one half whole wheat pita bread with 1 tablespoon part skim ricotta cheese and top with pear slices

- layer soft mini-corn flour tortillas with shredded low-fat cheddar cheese; roll up in aluminum foil and bake in 350°F toaster oven until cheese melts, about 5 minutes

- spread a brown rice cake with farmer cheese (similar to cottage cheese, but drier and firmer) and top with sliced fresh strawberries

- spread raisin toast with apple butter

- spread slices of whole-grain crisp bread (a wafer-thin cracker) with fruit-flavored low-fat yogurt

- try celery sticks stuffed with a mixture of peanut butter, chopped carrots, a dab of honey, and raisins

- make a fresh fruit sundae—top a ½ cup scoop of ice milk or frozen yogurt with crushed unsweetened fresh fruit mixed with a teaspoon of low-sugar strawberry jam

Sweet Potato Balls

Can't get your youngster interested in vegetables? Try sweet potatoes made this way. It will provide a good after-school energy boost.

Makes about 18 sweet potato balls

	Nonstick vegetable spray
2	**large sweet potatoes, boiled or baked and peeled, or a 1-pound can, drained well**
1	**8-ounce can crushed pineapples in their own juice**
1	**tablespoon margarine**
¼	**teaspoon salt**
½	**teaspoon cinnamon (optional)**
⅓	**cup cornflake crumbs**

1. Preheat oven to 400° F. Spray a cookie sheet with nonstick vegetable spray.

2. Mash sweet potatoes in a small mixing bowl. Drain crushed pineapple well, pressing out the juice.

3. Add pineapple, margarine, salt, and cinnamon to mashed sweet potato and mix well. Shape mixture into small balls and roll in cornflake crumbs.

4. Arrange balls on a greased cookie sheet and bake for 30 minutes. Serve warm or cold.

Preparation time: 20 minutes
Cooking time: 30 minutes
Nutrients per serving:
Calories: 40   Sat. fat: none
Total fat: less than   Cholesterol: none
   1 gm
            Percentage of calories from fat: 15

Pita Pizza

Here's an easy recipe that kids can make on their own after school. If your kids don't like the suggested vegetable toppings, go with what they like—broccoli, corn, spinach, sprouts, tomato slices. Anything goes.

Makes 4 pita pizzas

2 mini-sized pita breads (whole wheat or white)
6 tablespoons tomato sauce
2 mushrooms, sliced
8 thin slices zucchini
8 tablespoons grated part skim mozzarella cheese

1. Spread each pita half with tomato sauce. Add sliced mushrooms and zucchini. Spoon on cheese.

2. Heat the pitas in a toaster oven at 350° F for a few minutes or until the cheese melts and becomes nice and gooey.

Preparation time: 10 minutes
Cooking time: 3 minutes
Nutrients per serving:
   Calories: 130   Sat. fat: 1 gm
   Total fat: 3 gm   Cholesterol: 8 mg
         Percentage of calories from fat: 18

Mexican Bean Snack

Here's a good-tasting high-energy mini-meal for older chil-
dren with heartier appetites. The beans and whole wheat
muffin give a nice fiber boost.

Makes 4 servings

2   **whole wheat English muffins**
¼   **cup tomato puree**
¼   **cup canned kidney beans, drained and chopped**
1   **tablespoon chopped onion**
1   **tablespoon chopped green pepper**
½   **teaspoon dried oregano**
¼   **cup shredded part skim mozzarella cheese**
¼   **cup shredded lettuce**

1. Split muffins in half; toast lightly.
2. Mix tomato puree, beans, onion, green pepper, and oregano. Spread on muffin halves.
3. Sprinkle with cheese and broil until cheese is bubbly, about 2 minutes.
4. Garnish with shredded lettuce.

Preparation time: 20 minutes
Cooking time: 2 minutes
Nutrients per serving:
   Calories: 95   Sat. fat: less than 1 gm
   Total fat: 2 gm   Cholesterol: 4 mg
         Percentage of calories from fat: 14

Oven-Baked French Fries

These fries are so delicious that the grown-ups might gobble them up before the kids get a chance at them.

Makes 4 servings

2   **large baking potatoes**
3   **tablespoons grated Parmesan cheese**
¼   **teaspoon paprika**
      Nonstick vegetable spray

1. Preheat oven to 425° F.
2. Under cold running water, scrub the potatoes and then pat dry. Cut potatoes lengthwise into thin wedges.
3. In a plastic bag, mix Parmesan cheese and paprika. Then add the sliced potatoes, a few at a time in the bag; toss to coat wedges. Spray cookie sheet with nonstick vegetable spray; place potato pieces in a single layer and bake for 25 to 30 minutes or until crisp.
Serve plain or with salsa.

Preparation time: 10 minutes
Baking time: 30 minutes
Nutrients per serving:
   Calories: 101   Sat. fat: less than 1 gm
    Total fat: 1 gm   Cholesterol: 3 mg
          Percentage of calories from fat: 11

Spinach Dip

This colorful dip is a surefire way to get your youngster to gobble up veggies.

Serve with lots of carrot slices, red pepper strips, and jicama (pronounced hick-ah-mah*) cut up into shoestring sticks. Jicama is a Mexican potato that looks like a turnip and tastes like a water chestnut, only sweeter.*

Makes 2 cups

1   **10-ounce package frozen chopped spinach, thawed**
1   **cup light sour cream**
½   **cup low-fat yogurt**
1   **cup fresh parsley, loosely packed**
4   **scallions, white part only**
4   **whole water chestnuts, drained**
    Salt and freshly ground pepper to taste

1. To remove liquid from chopped spinach, squeeze by hand or wrap in paper towels and squeeze.

2. In a food processor or blender, mix together spinach, sour cream, yogurt, parsley, scallions, water chestnuts, and salt and pepper to taste. Cover and refrigerate.

Preparation time: 15 minutes, plus 4 hours chilling
Nutrients per serving:
  Calories: 29   Sat. fat: less than 1 gm
  Total fat: 1 gm   Cholesterol: 4 mg
            Percentage of calories from fat: 39

Fruity Popcorn

This nutritious popcorn should keep your youngster happy while she watches her favorite video.

Makes 8 1-cup servings

1   **tablespoon margarine, melted**
½   **teaspoon cinnamon**
8   **cups popped corn (popped without fat)**
1   **cup dried fruit bits**

1. Combine margarine and cinnamon, stir well.
2. Drizzle over popped corn, tossing gently to coat.
3. Add dried fruit and toss gently. Store in airtight container.

Preparation time: 10 minutes
Nutrients per serving:

Calories: 82	Sat. fat: none
Total fat: 2 gm	Cholesterol: none

Percentage of calories from fat: 18

Gingersnap Sandwiches

Gingersnaps are low in fat—so is the 1 percent low-fat cottage cheese. If Mom makes the filling, kids should enjoy making the sandwiches themselves for an after-school snack.

Makes 15 sandwiches

1   medium-size apple
½   cup 1 percent cottage cheese
2   tablespoons sugar
30   gingersnaps

1. Core apple and shred in food processor using the metal blade; set aside.
2. Blend cottage cheese in processor until smooth. Blend in apple and sugar. Using rubber spatula, spread apple filling onto flat side of cookie, topping each with another gingersnap to make a sandwich.

Preparation time: 10 minutes
Nutrients per sandwich:

Calories: 57	Sat. fat: less than 1 gm
Total fat: 1 gm	Cholesterol: less than 1 mg

Percentage of calories from fat: 21

Apple-Raspberry Chill

When my son-in-law was a little boy growing up in Baltimore, this was a favorite after-school snack. Sometimes he enjoyed it for dessert with an oatmeal cookie.

Makes 8 servings

1   3-ounce box raspberry-flavored gelatin
1   cup boiling water
1   15-ounce jar unsweetened applesauce
1½ teaspoons lemon juice
½   teaspoon cinnamon
    Banana slices or kiwi slices, for garnish

1. Add gelatin to 1 cup boiling water; stir until completely dissolved.

2. Stir in applesauce, lemon juice, and cinnamon.

3. Chill about 2 hours or until firm. Garnish with sliced bananas or kiwi.

Preparation time: 10 minutes, plus 2 hours chilling time
Nutrients per serving:
   Calories: 63   Sat. fat: none
   Total fat: none   Cholesterol: none
           Percentage of calories from fat: 0

Fresh Fruit Sipper

On a warm spring day, serve this after-school smoothie when your youngster brings home a few pals.

Makes 4 servings

1 pint vanilla ice milk, slightly softened
1 cup skim milk
1 small banana, cut into chunks

1. In a blender container, place ice milk, skim milk, and banana chunks. Cover and blend until smooth. Pour into glasses.

Preparation time: 5 minutes
Nutrients per serving:
    Calories: 139   Sat. fat: 2 gm
    Total fat: 3 gm   Cholesterol: 10 mg
             Percentage of calories from fat: 20

Orange Yogurt Pops

*Late for a scout meeting or soccer practice? With these pops
in the freezer, your youngster can grab a homemade orange-
yogurt pop and be on his or her way.*

Makes 8 pops

2   **cups vanilla low-fat yogurt**
1   **6-ounce can frozen orange juice concentrate,
        slightly defrosted**
1½ **tablespoons sugar, optional**
8   **waxed-paper cups (4-ounce size)**
16   **seedless grapes, halved**
8   **pop sticks**

1. Combine the yogurt, orange juice concentrate, and
sugar; stir until concentrate melts and sugar is dissolved.
Pour into paper cups, dividing evenly.
2. Drop handful of grape pieces into each cup. Freeze
until almost firm. Insert stick in center of each cup. Cover
cups with plastic wrap and freeze for a few hours or until
solid. To serve, peel off paper cup.

Preparation time: 10 minutes
Freezing time: overnight
Nutrients per serving:
    Calories: 85   Sat. fat: less than 1 gm
    Total fat: less than   Cholesterol: 3 mg
    1 gm
             Percentage of calories from fat: 10

PARTY AND HOLIDAY FOODS

Birthday parties and holidays are times of celebration—and great opportunities for eating high-fat sugar-laden foods. The occasional splurge isn't going to undo a year's worth of healthy eating, but many children attend lots of birthday parties. Surely, it makes sense to offer special treats that are lower in fat than traditional party fare. Try the scrumptious recipes in this section—we promise that no one will feel deprived.

Vegetable Pizza

Instead of overloading kids with cake and ice cream, try serving this pizza instead—it's chock-full of vitamin-packed veggies and moderate in fat. It's even better when you make your own pizza crust (you can sneak a little oat bran into the dough). But for convenience, packages of refrigerated dough available at supermarkets will do just fine. If you make the sauce in advance, this treat is quick to prepare for party dinners.

Makes 16 slices

Refrigerated pizza dough (enough for 2
　　pizzas)
1　cup chopped onion
2　cloves garlic, minced
2　tablespoons olive oil
1　28-ounce can tomatoes, chopped and undrained
2　8-ounce cans tomato sauce
2　tablespoons fresh minced parsley
2　teaspoons dried basil
1　teaspoon sugar
½　teaspoon oregano
¼　teaspoon pepper
　　Nonstick vegetable spray
Toppings
1　medium zucchini, sliced thin
1　large red pepper, cut into strips
1　cup thinly sliced fresh mushrooms
　　8 ounces (2 cups) shredded low-moisture, part
　　　skim mozzarella cheese
2　tablespoons grated Parmesan cheese

1. Prepare pizza dough according to package directions.
2. For sauce, sauté onion and garlic in oil, stirring frequently until onion is limp. Add tomatoes, tomato sauce, parsley, basil, sugar, oregano, and pepper. Simmer uncovered for about 1 hour or until thick. Allow to cool. (Can be made in advance and refrigerated.)
3. Meanwhile, preheat oven to 425° F. Spray 2 12-inch pizza pans with nonstick vegetable spray. Set aside.
4. Transfer dough to pans, following package directions and forming a flat pizza crust. Pinch edges to form a rim. Prick bottom and sides with fork.
5. Bake dough for 6 to 8 minutes or until dough is golden brown. Remove from oven and cool for 5 minutes.
6. Spread half of sauce evenly over each crust. Arrange zucchini slices, pepper strips, and mushroom slices on top.
7. Sprinkle with mozzarella and Parmesan cheeses.
8. Bake for 12 to 15 minutes or until cheese is bubbly and highly browned.

Preparation time: 30 minutes
Cooking time: 1 hour for sauce
Baking time: 30 minutes
Nutrients per serving:
  Calories: 178   Sat. fat: 1 gm
  Total fat: 5 gm   Cholesterol: 8 mg
      Percentage of calories from fat: 28

Heart-Smart Lasagna

Here's a low-fat lasagna dish with lots of vegetables and flavor. This is a good dish to make in advance and freeze for a birthday party or family gathering. If you have leftover sauce, freeze and serve with pasta for a quick lunch or dinner. Serve with garlic bread and tossed salad.

Makes 12 servings

¾   pound ground round
    Salt, pepper, fennel seeds, dash of hot pepper
      flakes, to taste
¼   cup olive oil
1½ cups onion, diced
2   cloves garlic, minced
2   carrots, peeled and chopped
1   celery stalk, chopped
1   medium green pepper, diced
½   pound mushrooms, sliced
1   cup dry red wine or chicken broth
1   35-ounce can plum tomatoes
2   16-ounce cans tomato sauce
1   6-ounce can tomato paste
2   teaspoons dried basil
2   teaspoons dried oregano
¼   cup minced fresh parsley
1   pound lasagna noodles
8   ounces part skim milk ricotta cheese
4   ounces grated Parmesan cheese
    Skim milk
8   ounces part skim milk mozzarella cheese,
      grated

1. In a skillet over medium heat, sauté ground round, breaking it up in pieces, until it is no longer pink. Drain off all grease. Season to taste with salt, pepper, fennel seeds, and a dash of hot pepper flakes. Set aside.

2. In a large saucepan, heat the oil and sauté onion, garlic, carrot, celery, and green pepper. Cook over medium heat until carrots are tender, about 15 to 20 minutes. Add mushrooms and sauté another 5 minutes. Add wine or broth and cook about 5 minutes. Add ground round, plum tomatoes broken up, tomato sauce, tomato paste, basil, oregano, and parsley. Simmer 2 hours, stirring occasionally.

3. Cook lasagna noodles in boiling salted water until tender but still firm. You do not need to use oil to prevent noodles from sticking together if you occasionally stir the noodles gently. Drain, rinse with cold water, and separate noodles.

4. Combine ricotta and half of the Parmesan cheese, thinning with skim milk to make a smooth paste.

5. Preheat oven to 350° F. Into a 9-by-13-inch pan, spoon a thin layer of sauce and cover with a layer of lasagna noodles. Place a layer of grated mozzarella and ricotta-Parmesan mixture on top. Add some more sauce. Continue, using all ingredients, ending with a layer of noodles. Top with sauce and a sprinkling of the second portion of the ricotta-Parmesan mixture.

6. Bake for about 25 minutes. Remove and let stand for 10 minutes before cutting.

Preparation time: 35 minutes
Cooking time: 2 hours
Baking time: 30 minutes
Nutrients per serving:
  Calories: 425   Sat. fat: 7 gm
  Total fat: 16 gm   Cholesterol: 41 mg
        Percentage of calories from fat: 34

Cheesy Pretzels

Here's a non-sugary recipe for a Halloween or a birthday party; your kids will have a ball helping you twist the dough into pretzels.

Makes 33 pretzels

1   tablespoon active dry yeast
1   teaspoon salt
1   tablespoon sugar
1½ cups warm water
3½ cups flour
1   cup calorie-reduced grated cheddar cheese
2   egg whites, slightly beaten
2   tablespoons grated Parmesan cheese, optional

1. Preheat oven to 425° F. Dissolve yeast, salt, and sugar in water in food processor bowl. Add flour and cheddar cheese.

2. Mix by turning processor on-off a few times. Then run about 1 minute to knead the dough until smooth. (If dough sticks, add more flour.)

3. Remove dough and form into a log. Cut into 33 pieces. Roll each piece into a rope 14 inches long. Let dough rest 5 minutes. Twist into pretzel shape. Place on ungreased cookie sheet. Brush with egg white and sprinkle on Parmesan cheese, if desired. Bake 15 to 18 minutes or until golden.

Preparation time: 30 minutes
Cooking time: 16 minutes
Nutrients per serving:
  Calories: 63   Sat. fat: less than 1 gm
  Total fat: less than   Cholesterol: 3 mg
    1 gm
            Percentage of calories from fat: 10

Chocolate Birthday Cake

The secret to this deliciously moist chocolate cake is the (believe it or not) low-fat buttermilk! It lends a richness without extra fat.

Makes 16 servings

2   cups sifted unbleached flour
1⅓ cups granulated sugar
½   cup unsweetened cocoa
2   teaspoons baking soda
1   teaspoon baking powder
¼   teaspoon salt
1   cup low-fat buttermilk
⅔   cup canola oil
2   teaspoons vanilla
1   cup orange juice
     Confectioners' sugar, for garnish

1. Preheat oven to 350° F.
2. Grease and flour a 9-cup tube pan or baking pan.
3. In a large bowl, combine the flour, sugar, cocoa, baking soda, baking powder, and salt.
4. Make a well in the center and using a wooden spoon, stir in buttermilk, oil, and vanilla. Stir in orange juice.
5. Pour batter into prepared pan and bake for 60 to 70 minutes, or until tester when inserted comes out clean.
6. Cool on wire rack 15 to 20 minutes, then invert cake onto rack and allow to cool completely. Dust with confectioners' sugar shaken through wire strainer, if desired.

Preparation time: 20 minutes
Baking time: 60 to 70 minutes
Nutrients per serving:
   Calories: 219   Sat. fat: less than 1 gm
   Total fat: 10 gm   Cholesterol: 61 mg
           Percentage of calories from fat: 40

"Half the Fat" Carrot Cake

The following recipe was a big hit at a Grandpa's sixtieth birthday party where lots of little kids enjoyed the cake as much as the health-conscious grown-ups. The cake has only 9 grams of fat per serving; an equal size serving of a traditional cream cheese–topped carrot cake has a whopping 32 grams of fat!

Makes 16 servings

2	cups shredded carrots
¾	cup golden raisins
½	cup canola or corn oil
2	teaspoons vanilla extract
1	8½-ounce can peaches with "lite" syrup
5	egg whites
3	cups unbleached flour
2½	teaspoons baking soda
1½	cups sugar
3	teaspoons cinnamon
½	teaspoon salt, optional
4	ounces Neufchatel or "lite" cream cheese
1	teaspoon vanilla
2	cups confectioners' sugar
	Granny Bear cookies for garnish, optional

1. Preheat oven to 350° F.
2. To prepare cake, in a food processor combine carrots, raisins, oil, vanilla, peaches and syrup, and egg whites. Using the metal blade, process until well blended.
3. In a large mixing bowl, sift together flour, baking soda, sugar, cinnamon, and salt, if desired.
4. Add carrot mixture to dry ingredients and beat until well blended.
5. Pour into two 9-inch lightly oiled cake pans. Bake 40 minutes or until cake tester comes out clean. Set aside to cool.

6. To prepare icing, blend together Neufchatel or "lite" cream cheese, vanilla, and confectioners' sugar. Frost only the middle and top layers of the cake. Decorate with miniature Granny Bear cookies, if desired.

Preparation time: 20 minutes
Baking time: 40 minutes
Nutrients per serving:
  Calories: 312   Sat. fat: 2 gm
  Total fat: 9 gm   Cholesterol: 6 mg
            Percentage of calories from fat: 25

Mini-Chocolate Cupcakes

Younger children will love these tiny chocolate treats.

Makes 24 mini-cupcakes

For Cupcakes
1½ cups unbleached flour
1   cup sugar
¼   cup unsweetened cocoa powder
1   teaspoon baking soda
½   teaspoon salt
1   cup water
¼   cup plus 2 tablespoons canola oil
1   tablespoon vinegar
1   teaspoon vanilla
    Nonstick vegetable spray
For Chocolate Glaze
1   tablespoon nonfat yogurt
2 to 3 tablespoons unsweetened cocoa powder
½   teaspoon water
¾   cup sifted confectioners' sugar
2   tablespoons colored sprinkles, optional

1. Preheat oven to 375° F. Combine flour, sugar, cocoa, baking soda, and salt in medium-size mixing bowl. Add water, oil, vinegar, and vanilla. Beat mixture with a wooden spoon until batter is smooth and ingredients well blended.

2. Coat 2 mini-muffin tins with nonstick spray; dust with flour. Pour batter into muffin tins, filling almost to the top. Bake for about 15 to 16 minutes or until tester inserted in center comes out clean.

3. Remove muffins to wire rack. Cool completely before adding chocolate glaze to tops of muffins.

4. To make chocolate glaze, add yogurt, cocoa powder, and water to confectioners' sugar. Mix until frosting is well blended and smooth. Spread on top of cupcakes. Garnish with sprinkles, if desired.

Preparation time: 20 minutes
Baking time: 16 minutes
Nutrients per serving:
   Calories: 108   Sat. fat: less than 1 gm
   Total fat: 4 gm   Cholesterol: less than 1 mg
          Percentage of calories from fat: 30

Crunchy Fruit and Chocolate Drops

Here's a high-fiber sweet for special parties; great for Halloween parties, too.

Makes 40 drops

6   ounces Swiss milk chocolate
1   cup Corn Chex
½   cup toasted oat cereal
½   cup golden raisins
⅓   cup crushed peanuts

1. Place chocolate in top of a double boiler; bring water to a boil. Stir until chocolate melts. Remove from heat; add cereals, raisins, and nuts, stirring mixture well.

2. Drop mixture by heaping teaspoonfuls onto a waxed paper-lined baking sheet. Chill.

Preparation time: 30 minutes
Nutrients per cookie:
   Calories: 39   Sat. fat: less than 1 gm
   Total fat: 2 gm   Cholesterol: none
         Percentage of calories from fat: 44

Crispy Crunch Bars

Kids love this confection and it's easy to make.

Makes 24 bars

    Nonstick vegetable spray
3   **cups tiny marshmallows**
3   **tablespoons margarine**
½   **teaspoon vanilla**
5   **cups toasted oat cereal**
½   **cup raisins**
½   **cup sunflower seeds**

1. Line a 13-by-9-by-2-inch baking pan with foil. Spray with nonstick vegetable spray. In a large saucepan, heat marshmallows and margarine over low heat, stirring constantly until marshmallows are melted. Remove from heat.

2. Stir in vanilla. Stir in half of the cereal at a time.

3. Fold in raisins and sunflower seeds. Turn mixture into prepared pans. Press evenly with back of wooden spoon. Cool. Cut into bars.

Preparation time: 30 minutes, plus cooling time.
Nutrients per cookie:
   Calories: 76   Sat. fat: less than 1 gm
   Total fat: 3 gm   Cholesterol: none
         Percentage of calories from fat: 37

Defatted Pumpkin Pie

It's hard not to go overboard on fat at the Thanksgiving groaning board. You can minimize the damage by serving this delicious pumpkin pie, made with evaporated skim milk and a gingersnap crust.

Makes 8 servings

1   cup crushed gingersnaps (about 16 cookies)
2½   tablespoons margarine
3   tablespoons granulated sugar
½   cup packed light brown sugar
1½   tablespoons unbleached white flour
1¼   teaspoons cinnamon
½   teaspoon mace
¼   teaspoon ground cloves
2   large egg whites, lightly beaten
1   16-ounce can solid-packed pumpkin (not
          pumpkin filling)
1   12-ounce can evaporated skim milk
½   teaspoon vanilla extract

1. Preheat oven to 375° F.

2. To prepare crust: process gingersnaps in a blender or food processor. Melt the margarine and blend well with cookie crumbs.

3. Using your fingers, press the crumb mixture into an 8-inch pie pan, forming an even layer over the bottom and sides of the pan to within ½ inch of the rim. Bake in a 375°F oven for about 8 minutes; remove and cool on a rack.

4. To prepare filling, combine sugars, flour, cinnamon, mace, and cloves. Add the beaten egg whites and pumpkin puree, stirring until well blended.

5. Add milk and vanilla to the mixture a little at a time, mixing until the filling is completely smooth. Pour filling into the cooled pie crust, smoothing the mixture to the ends of pie evenly. Bake in 375°F oven for about 50 minutes or until the center of the filling appears set when the pan is jiggled slightly. Cool on rack.

Preparation time: 35 minutes
Cooking time: 60 minutes
Nutrients per serving:

Calories: 228	Sat. fat: 1 gm
Total fat: 5 gm	Cholesterol: 7 mg
	Percentage of calories from fat: 20

Vegetable Tzimmis

Tzimmis *means a medley; carrot and sweet potato tzimmis
was always a traditional Passover dish in our home, usually
made with fatty meats and chicken fat! A delicious low-fat
version is offered here. My daughter Kimberly likes this
defatted dish better.*

Makes 4 servings

1   **teaspoon each peanut oil and margarine**
½   **cup onion, chopped**
½   **cup red pepper, chopped**
¼   **cup celery, diced**
¼   **cup carrot, diced**
1   **tablespoon fresh parsley, chopped**
1   **tablespoon fresh dill, chopped**
¼   **teaspoon each salt and pepper**
½   **cup hot chicken stock, defatted**
2   **tablespoons walnuts, chopped**
2   **each pitted dates and apricot halves, sliced**
2   **tablespoons golden raisins**
6   **ounces cooked sweet potatoes, pared and cubed
       (about 1 large potato)**

1. In a 10-inch nonstick skillet, combine oil and margarine
and heat until margarine melts.

2. Add onion, pepper, celery and carrot, parsley, dill,
salt, and pepper. Stir to combine.

3. Cook over medium-high heat, stirring occasionally
until crisp and tender, about 3 to 5 minutes.

4. Add chicken stock, stir to combine, and bring mixture to a boil. Add walnuts, dates, apricots, and raisins to vegetable mixture and stir to combine.

5. Reduce heat to low and let simmer until flavors blend and fruits are softened, about 8 minutes. Remove from heat and fold in potatoes.

Preparation time: 20 minutes
Cooking time: 25 minutes
Nutrients per serving:
   Calories: 150   Sat. fat: less than 1 gm
   Total fat: 5 gm   Cholesterol: none
          Percentage of calories from fat: 28

Pineapple Cheesecake Squares

Rich desserts are a must to end Easter Sunday dinner. Here's a delicious cheesecake with one fourth the fat of traditional cheesecakes, and 80 percent less cholesterol. The cake is cut in squares; for little ones, cut into quarters.

Makes 24 servings

2   cups graham cracker crumbs
3   tablespoons honey
½   teaspoon cinnamon
1½ tablespoons canola oil
    Nonstick vegetable spray
1   8-ounce tub cream-style farmer's cheese and 8 ounces light cream cheese, room temperature
½   cup sugar
5   egg whites
1   teaspoon vanilla
⅔   cup unsweetened pineapple juice
¼   cup flour
¼   cup sugar
1   20-ounce can crushed pineapple in juice, reserve juice

1. Preheat oven to 350° F.

2. To make crust, in a food processor, blend graham cracker crumbs, honey, cinnamon, and oil. Press firmly into a 9-by-13-inch pan, sprayed with nonstick vegetable spray.

3. To make filling, whip together until smooth the cheeses, sugar, egg white, vanilla, and pineapple juice in a clean bowl of food processor.

4. Pour cheese mixture over crust. Bake 25 to 30 minutes or until center is set. Cool.

5. To make topping, combine flour, sugar and reserved pineapple juice to equal one cup.

6. Over medium heat, bring to a boil and stir for 1 minute, until mixture reaches a thick pudding consistency. Remove from heat, fold in crushed pineapple, and allow to cool.

7. Spread pineapple mixture over cheese mixture. Cover loosely and refrigerate for about 4 hours. Cut into 24 squares.

Preparation time: 25 minutes
Baking time: 35 minutes (plus 4 hours to set)
Nutrients per square:
  Calories: 144   Sat. fat: 1 gm
  Total fat: 4 gm   Cholesterol: 11 mg
            Percentage of calories from fat: 29

Recipe Index